Wicked

Puritans

OF ESSEX COUNTY

Wicked
Puritans
OF ESSEX COUNTY

Tom Juergens

Charleston   London

THE
History
PRESS

Published by The History Press
Charleston, SC 29403
www.historypress.net

First published 2011

Manufactured in the United States

ISBN 978.1.59629.566.7

Library of Congress Cataloging-in-Publication Data

Juergens, Tom.
Wicked Puritans of Essex County / Tom Juergens.
p. cm.
Includes bibliographical references.
ISBN 978-1-59629-566-7
1. Puritans--Massachusetts--Essex County--History--17th century. 2. Puritans--
Massachusetts--Essex County--Biography. 3. Essex County (Mass.)--History--17th century.
4. Essex County (Mass.)--Church history--17th century. 5. Essex County (Mass.)--Social
conditions--17th century. 6. Essex County (Mass.)--Biography. 7. Violence--Massachusetts-
-Essex County--History--17th century. 8. Corruption--Massachusetts--Essex County--
History--17th century. I. Title.
F72.E7J84 2011
2010052257

For the always cheerful Michelle,
wife and ally,
with whom all things become possible.

Contents

Acknowledgements

H eartfelt thanks to everyone who offered information, insight, guidance, encouragement and reviews during the research and writing of this book. This includes everyone who was or is in my writing groups; the staffs at the American Antiquarian Society, the Massachusetts Historical Society and the Massachusetts Archives; and the librarians at the following libraries: Hamilton-Wenham, Ipswich, Beverly, Peabody Institute, Boston, Philips, Essex County Law and Social Law. I am also grateful for inspiration from friends and colleagues, including those who might mistakenly think they are forgotten. And, more than ever, for family members, immediate and otherwise. You all inspire and mean more to the lonely writer than can easily be put into words.

Introduction

The people in this book are not the sorts of characters usually found in books about colonial Massachusetts. They are mean and sneaky, deceptive and deadly. They are cheats, slavers and drunks. They are baby killers and viciously creative abusers of children, servants, animals and each other. They are long dead but are resurrected here to prove a point: all was not well in the New World, and there never was any such thing as "the good old days," really.

This book is not about the Pilgrims, who broke clean from the Church of England and came off the *Mayflower* in Plymouth in 1620. It is about the Puritans, who came in a fleet of ships and landed in Boston and points north, including Salem, ten years later. The Puritans were more numerous, better educated and better off financially than the Pilgrims and had not left the church but sought to purify it from within. With a vengeance, as it turned out.

But first, a quick detour into the nature of early histories about the Massachusetts Bay Colony.

Before the word *ethnocentric* was coined, there was a tradition among old-time Massachusetts historians, an unspoken agreement to play up the colonists' nobler qualities. That helped maintain the notion, quite appealing to the colonists' descendants, those very historians among them, that if you could trace your lineage back to them, you had historical bragging rights, which came with a certain pedigree. Maybe even some sort of tacit superiority, however subtle and undefined, or at least as legitimate a claim to superiority as has ever been allowed by such a collection of egalitarians as Americans. The blueblood, eastern snob archetype had to start somewhere. And if there ever was any superiority, was it not logical that it stemmed from the colonists themselves, who were tough, stern and forbidding, yes, but also a notch above common human messiness and corruption, right? Somehow inherently *good*, if not better. That much was in a grade school lesson one day, wasn't it?

The current fashion for historians is to find and explore cracks in veneers, to turn mythic, idealized stereotypes over and poke their underbellies in search of the gritty stuff. And the most direct way to do that with the Essex Puritans is to read their criminal record—the *Records and Files of the Quarterly Courts of Essex County*, covering 1635 to 1685—which is the foundation of this book. Information from the *Records and Files* and from *Records of the Court of Assistants*,[1] the high court in Boston for the most serious trials, is referred to in this book as simply "the record" or "the criminal record." Excerpts from the Essex courts appear in unattributed quotes throughout. Quotes from the high court, and from other sources, are either immediately identified or in the endnotes, or both. When something's worth is estimated, its value comes from contemporary probate records. Some quotes from individuals are rough going, antiquated and obscure, but there is real humanity in them—at times you can almost see the court clerks shaking their heads as they record the proceedings. And for anyone linguistically inclined, it's worth a cyber visit to the record for a taste of genuine colonial English.

The *Records and Files'* nine volumes (over four thousand pages) reaffirm two things. First, the leaders of a theocracy will consider themselves God's elect and will redefine what wickedness, intolerance and authority are all about. Second, the rank and file will live up to all the wickedness expected of it. Puritan judges, particularly big on authority, enjoyed the honorific "worshipful" and tolerated neither backtalk nor disparagement, in or out of court. In 1668, Thomas Wells, a ship's carpenter, compared the Ipswich magistrates and court to "the Inquisition house in Spain, [where] when a man is once brought into court he [knows] not for what [and is] as good [as] hanged," and got arrested for saying so.

The record's rainbow of criminality scuttles any romantic notions about Puritan "purity" being a given, about the colonial period as a particularly virtuous time or about young Essex County—or anywhere in New England—as some bucolic nirvana where morality reigned supreme. Michael Zuckerman put it well in *Peaceable Kingdoms*:

Like any artifact of the imagination, the archetypical New England town has been tied only tenuously to the actual one. Its inhabitants have been reduced to caricatures of stolid virtue, folkloric figures impossible to conceive sniffling through the dismal winters or fornicating out back in the barn. To the local historians of New England, the town and its town meeting have always been more nearly objects of reverence than of research.[2]

Not everyone under Puritan rule was a Puritan, but the record makes no distinctions, and the courts certainly didn't. But the majority of seventeenth-century Essex County residents were Puritans and tried, well, puritanically, if not quixotically, to live faultless, saintly lives. They are nearly as famous for that striving as their government was for its abhorrence of human frailty. The definition of wickedness changes over time, and this book casts the net wide to catch it in all its incarnations, old and new. It does that by including things that were once considered normal and are now considered wicked, or at least wrong, like slavery and corporal punishment, and by also including things that were once considered wicked and are now considered normal, like dancing and singing or wearing something extra nice. Back then, morality applied by law to just about everything, was policed by just about everyone and was consequently found to be transgressed just about everywhere. The morality crusade reached into the woods, orchards and fields; was carried to hearths and bedrooms; and justified peeping in others' windows. Life was an unending opportunity to fall from grace, whether failing to aid a stranger in need or missing church, both chargeable offenses. Enforcing the code was a duty eagerly undertaken. Breaking it brought on everything from minor annoyances to one or more circles of hell.

Western Essex was frontier. Its eastern, coastal edge was a bustling, rough-and-tumble, land-and-sea corridor where you could run into some tough characters. A tally of criminal prosecutions in the neighboring counties of Essex (home to Salem) and Suffolk (home to Boston) from 1671 to 1674 shows that in certain respects Essex could take the lead in wickedness. In those years, Essex had more prosecutions for fornication (forty-eight versus forty-six), far more cases of drunkenness (twenty-three versus fourteen), far more breaches of the peace (thirty-two versus nine), one more case of abusing a constable (seven), more prosecutions of swearing (nine versus five) and only two fewer cases of stealing (thirty-six). But maybe there were more constables and informers per capita in Essex, making it harder to get away with anything. Or maybe Essex was wilder, a little rougher around the edges.

Throughout this book, "Essex" refers to the county, not the Town of Essex, which incorporated from Ipswich, Salem and Andover in 1819. Ipswich and Salem covered vast swaths of the present-day county. The early Essex towns were Gloucester (1623), Salem (1626), Lynn (established in 1629, so named in 1637), Ipswich (1634), Marblehead and Newbury (1635), Wenham (1638), Rowley (1639), Haverhill and Salisbury (1640), Manchester (by-the-Sea, 1645) and Andover (1646). Topsfield was incorporated in 1650. Later incorporations created the other Essex towns: from Salisbury came Amesbury (1666) and from Amesbury came Merrimac (1876). From Salem came Beverly (1668) and Danvers (1757). From Danvers came Peabody (1855). From Rowley came Boxford (1685), Bradford (1668, from which came Groveland in 1850 and later became part of Haverhill) and Georgetown (1838). From Haverhill came Methuen (1725). From Andover (and Methuen) came Lawrence (1847). From Salem, Topsfield, Andover and other towns came Middleton (1728). From Newbury came Newburyport (1764) and West Newbury (1819). From Ipswich came Hamilton (1793) and the aforementioned Town of Essex in 1819. From Lynn came Lynnfield (1814), Nahant (1853), Saugus (1815) and Swampscott (1852). From Gloucester came Rockport (1840) and from Andover came North Andover (1855). Another geographical point regards the term "the eastward," which crops up here and there and refers to what is now Maine, sailed to on the downwind tack due to prevailing westerlies and thus called "the eastward," or "down east."

There are a few things to keep in mind when reading stories based on court records. The Puritans were as capable as anyone of baseless allegations, lies, spite, vendettas, revenge and economic attacks. None of that can be discounted when considering the testimony of defendants, witnesses or "prosecutors," who were simply aggrieved citizens representing themselves. Many people appeared for "presentments" only, merely to face a charge; their cases nonetheless add to this book's statistics. Also, the record is egregiously short on details, including punishments, just when you're good and tantalized and want to know more. Even some major cases are described in brief and recorded without final outcomes. Numerous brief mentions— quick detours into mere snippets of wickedness—are included because they are just too interesting to leave out; thanks are offered for bearing with the staccato rhythm they sometimes engender.

It should also be remembered that *Records and Files of the Quarterly Courts of Essex County* is *printed*. It is a reproduction—and a partial interpretation—of

Early Essex County when it reached into current-day New Hampshire and most towns were coastal. From *Crime and Punishment in Early Massachusetts 1620–1692* (Boston: Beacon Press, 1966) by Edwin Powers. *Courtesy Beacon Press.*

the original handwritten court records, which are long gone. The originals were transcribed and abstracted by Harriet S. Tapley. Tapley's work was then edited by George Francis Dow, so not all quotes from the record are necessarily from the original court clerks but may be from Tapley and Dow, who quoted and paraphrased the clerks and added commentary as they saw fit. Tapley and Dow remained faithful, however, to the fact that words and names in the original were written in wildly inconsistent phonetic forms, even on the same page, and even when they refer to one and the same thing. They did that by leaving them alone. For clarity's sake, those inconsistencies have been, for the most part, made uniform and modernized.

Not modernized, to date, is human nature, which is immune to time.

Here, then, is just how similar many among the Puritans were to many among us, and we to them. This you can see whether you read every word or open to random pages.

At nearly every turn, there we are.

Wicked Deeds and
Dire Consequences

Before getting to individual cases, the fascination with cruelty dictates an overview of Puritan crime and punishment. Puritan sentences were indeed harsh, sometimes downright medieval. Many would qualify today as cruel and unusual, or downright torture, and themselves constitute their own category of wickedness. At the time, of course, they were normal. For instance, the punishment for Thomas West, caught burglarizing and stealing on the Lord's Day in 1657, shows his draconian treatment *and* implies he got off easy.

"This being his first offence, he was ordered to be branded in the forehead with a 'B' and have one of his ears cut off," the record matter-of-factly states. That's "B" as in burglar, branded as in forever.

Other indications of Puritan severity are the number and types of crimes that could lead to the gallows.

Capital religious crimes included: idolatry, or the worship of any god but the Puritans' God; blasphemy, or the denial of God altogether (Indians were added as potential blasphemers in 1646); heresy; witchcraft; and "defiance" by Jesuits and Quakers, who risked death when they openly disagreed with Puritan orthodoxy.

Political loyalty was enforced by making a capital crime of conspiracy, and of rebellion, which applied to towns and forts as well as governments. Piracy was a hanging offense, as was mutiny, which applied to churches as well as vessels. (Maritime crimes were prosecuted in Boston and, with one exception, are not in this book because they did not occur in the county proper.) Treason against the king, and military service with foreign states allied against the king or the king's allies, was also punishable by death.

Lying (bearing false witness) in a capital case was deadly dangerous. Cursing or smiting parents was a crime fatal to those sixteen or older on paper but was rarely fully prosecuted and did not apply if the parents were negligent in education or if there was provocation, namely "extreme and cruel correction" to the degree that threatened death or maiming. The capital crime of being a stubborn or rebellious son also applied to those sixteen or older, prosecutable only by testimony of the natural parents.

Capital sexual crimes included bestiality, the sentence for which included not just the execution of the offender but the slaying and burial—but not the eating—of the animal. Sodomy, any man lying with another "as he lyth with a woman," would put both parties to death unless one was forced, or under fourteen, in which case the punishment was severe anyway. (Appearances mattered. Two men, Thomas Beale and Richard Whitmarsh, were admonished in 1648, perhaps for idleness, perhaps for nonconformity; it is not specified. They are on record as having been seen "in the fields, near orchards, and lying on the ground, talking together.") Adultery was a capital offense but without much popular support; jurors often effectively forgave it by couching guilty verdicts in indirect, nonlethal terms. Rape was made a capital crime after its first occurrence in the colony in 1641, although it had long been a capital crime in England.

Burglary brought thieves to the gallows upon their third offense. The first got them branded and sometimes mutilated; the second got them another branding and a whipping.

Hangings naturally drew huge crowds. People traveled for miles and camped out for days to see the sights and mingle:

> A sermon immediately preceded the hanging and could last an hour. The final tableau on the scaffold might be one of high tragedy or low comedy, of great human dignity or common brutality. Reasonable requests by the condemned were indulged. The occasion was entirely novel for most of the participants, including the sheriff and hangman, who often had only oral tradition rather than established procedure to follow.[3]

Puritan judges were not entirely merciless, and not everyone found guilty of a capital crime was hanged. They would certainly get a whipping, though, and sit or stand at the gallows with a rope around their necks for an hour or two to show they *ought* to have died. Sometimes those lucky souls were also made to wear halters, like animals.

Whipping was by far the most common punishment, delivered like clockwork to transgressors of all stripes, even to those who stole a bit of milk or a handkerchief or were caught in idleness. Whipping, or "scourging," was usually carried out at a stationary whipping post, but the guilty might also be tied to a cart's tail and whipped while being paraded through the streets and/or out of the jurisdiction. In this book's half century, the tally of known whippings in Essex—whippings ordered without the option of paying a fine instead—was 185. That averages about 3.7 per year, or one nearly every time the quarterly court convened. (Courts were held, at first, in taverns, also called "ordinaries," or at someone's house.) To that average, add possible whippings, or whippings ordered with the option of paying a fine instead (193) *but not having the money*, and the chances of seeing a whipping somewhere in Essex every three months approached certainty. Because cases piled up waiting for the judges to arrive in any given town on the court circuit, there were doubtless days on which several whippings occurred in succession. For maximum effect, whippings were held on the Sabbath at the public meetinghouse in the town where the crime had occurred. Exceptions were made when the judges were so incensed they just couldn't wait.

Sixty-three of Essex's 185 known whippings were "severe," which is nowhere explicitly defined but in practice meant thirty or forty stripes and, from time to time, the instruction they be "well laid on." The Puritans followed Mosaic Code by limiting whippings to no more than forty strokes, which approaches lethality, and in practice delivered thirty-nine, as did the ancient Hebrews, to avoid the possibility of a miscount.[4] The force put into the lash was one variable. Another was the whip itself. In the case of one couple to be whipped for fornication, the court ordered that "the smart be taken off." Smarts—little pieces of bone or metal, or sometimes knots—are put into a whip to dig into flesh, giving us the phrase "that really smarts." Sometimes, for extra zing, smarts were soaked in salt water and dried so the absorbed salt could penetrate the wounds. Once in a great while, a whipping was ordered to be moderate, never anything less.

Whippings could stand alone or be augmented with branding, disenfranchisement (the deprivation of rights and privileges, usually the right to vote), jail time, humiliation, and mutilation or dismemberment, all of which could also stand alone. Mutilations and dismemberments were rare. The privilege of sentencing them, and of sentencing death or banishment, was the high court's. Puritans cut off ears and slit open nostrils but drew the line at chopping off hands and burning people at the stake; those were English practices they considered barbarous.

Creative pleadings—the more obsequious the better—got half a dozen whippings remitted, or "respited" (given respite from). In 1677, Lawrence Clenton and Mary Wooden, confessed fornicators, were whipped, he severely, but not by Constable Jonas Gregory, their first designated whipper. Gregory refused and was whipped himself "for abusing the court in not performing the duty of his office." Only one whipping was *not* carried out, when a Lynn constable let Anthony Ribeara walk away from the whipping post. Ribeara had stolen a coat. The Lynn constable's pity probably cost him his whipping fee, not to mention his office. Such fees, from the few recorded instances of their payment, included: twenty shillings per year, twelve shillings for whipping "several persons," ten shillings for whipping four people, thirty pence for a single whipping, forty shillings for "branding prisoners" and five shillings for one combination whipping-and-branding. Five shillings would buy a pair of boots, a brass kettle and skillet or a looking glass.

Only one person dared object out loud to all the whipping—William Young of Andover, who in 1655 called those who instituted it "rude, deboyst [debased] fellows." Young openly wished them all hanged, which got him cited for "abusive speeches." His punishment, if any, was not recorded.

All Puritan punishments were public, and every town had wooden stocks to hold people's feet (or bilboes, an iron bar and shackles that did the same). Pillories held the head and hands. The whole idea was to put the wicked on display where they could be not only hurt but humiliated and made sport of. Sabbath-breakers were put in cages to spend a few hours on display, as were drunks, like the woman lifted out of the street where "the hogs were tearing at her clothes." Another humiliation was wearing a letter—"A" for adultery, "V" for venality and so on—or wearing a sign that spelled out a particular wickedness. Essex used all these punishments and, perhaps, the ducking stool and the branks, an iron cage that went around the head with a spiked plate over the tongue, making it painful to speak. There is no mention of the ducking stool or the branks in the record, but lots of things went unrecorded in the 1600s. The tongues of Essex gossips, scolders and railers were silenced with the simpler, cheaper cleft stick—split wood that when opened pinches back, like a clothespin.

Corporal punishment was at least short-lived, compared to *any* jail time. Incarceration could turn lethal due to cold and disease, which was exacerbated by poor nutrition, vermin and the inconceivable lack of any accommodation for bodily functions. Many people, merely accused and waiting for trial, may have wished for a whipping if that would only get them released. Joseph Gatchell, petitioning the court for release in 1679, described jail as a "noisome place not fit for a Christian man to breath in" and a "hazard to…health and life…it being impossible that any human creature should endure to live in so pestiferous a stink."

Fashion Police, Humbugs and Party Poopers

Anything too much fun registered somewhere on the Puritan wickedness scale, even if it did rank low. Laws proscribing merriment and laxity were among the very first passed, and anyone who indulged in fashion, played games or got too idle or too jolly was fair game (Christmas was observed and decidedly not "celebrated").

Moderate drinking was fine at taverns and at home, but gatherings elsewhere, alcohol-fueled or not (cast as "disorderly meetings"), were suspect and subject to investigation, as were any displays of exuberance, in public or at home. Daniel Owls got a choice of a twenty-shilling fine or the stocks for "leaping and dancing" at his house in 1641. His resentment, for whatever reason, was recorded.

"I do not care for the best magistrates in the land," he declared. "If [I] met them in the field I should slash them, for I have been a pretty fellow in my time."

Dancing and singing while on watch "to the disturbance of several neighbors and witnesses" brought three men into court in 1668. In 1653, Thomas Wheller answered to "profane and foolish dancing, singing, and wanton speeches." The Puritans loved the word *wanton* and used it all the time, as it is the opposite of clean, decent, moral and righteous.

Cards and dice were illegal, as was shuffleboard (then "shovel board"). Playing games fell into the category of the "misspending of time," which was the twin brother of idleness. And there was to be no sitting around, either. Spending time "idly or unprofitably" was forbidden, and constables were ordered to take special note of "common coasters, unprofitable fowlers, and tobacco takers."

Bachelors were suspect almost by definition. To stay out of jail and not be run out of town, John Littleale of Haverhill, single and "illegally living alone, whereby he is subject to much sin and iniquity, which ordinarily are the companions and consequences of a solitary life," had to settle with "some orderly family in the town, and be subject to the orderly rules of family government." Idlers might have to report their weekly activities or take on court-ordered work. In 1699, Joshua Turland, "an idle and extravagant person" in danger of "falling into mischief," was overseen by the Beverly selectmen, who were to "put him out to service or otherwise dispose of him for his good and safety."

Idle strangers simply had no place. The aimless Simon Foster and his wife, up from Dedham and making a nuisance of themselves, were classified as "wandering, vagabond persons" and banished from the county. Simon was whipped out at a cart's tail. His wife rode in the cart, unwhipped "on account of her present illness, which is at least pretended."

Nobody, man or woman, could wear "new and immodest fashions." Fashion prosecutions were scarce until 1652 when, apparently, a shipment of

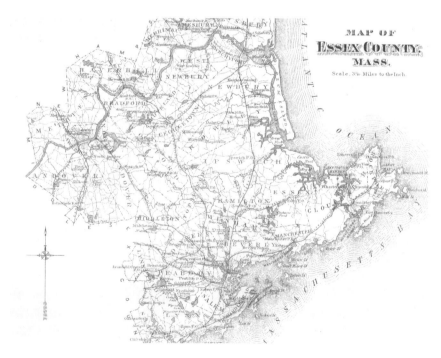

Essex County in 1878. From *History of Essex County Massachusetts: The Most Historic County in America* (Boston: C.F. Jewett & Company, 1878). *Courtesy Beverly Public Library.*

finery was landed somewhere nearby. There were twenty fashion defendants that year (eight the next, then only one or two a year). Exceptions were made for those "above the ordinary rank," which meant those with a proven minimum family value of £200, who were duly noted in several fashion prosecutions as those against whom charges were dismissed. John Chubb was not in that category. He was therefore admonished in 1675 for "excess in apparel, beyond that of a man of his degree." Illegal finery included lace, silver or gold threads, silk, tiffany hoods, points and ribbons, "broad lace" and "French fall" shoes. Jonas Fairbanks was presented for wearing "great boots" but was discharged without penalty, "it appearing he did not wear them after the law was published."

A 1682 warrant sought three women for "folding their hair, frizzling and knots, and wearing silk scarves."

Musical instruments get one mention, an enigmatic 1679 complaint about someone playing, or perhaps simply owning, a fiddle.

While the Puritans criminalized most pleasures, they prosecuted one above all others. The most universal, inescapable, obsessed-over and celebrated one. The one that today practically enjoys the status of a birthright.

Sex: The Good, the Bad and the Loathsome

The Puritans were not, as it turns out, all that puritanical about sex. In fact, they often characterized people and animals as "lusty" and discussed sex, and the lack of sex, frankly.

Sex within marriage was fine and good. What society could succeed without it? Sex and the marriage contract were very much the purview of civil authority, and it was not until 1692 that ministers' marriage ceremonies carried any legal weight. But for what came after a marriage, it was safest to stick to the straight and narrow. Why else would certain undefined acts result in the vague charge of "defiling the marriage bed" that some married couples faced?

What *wasn't* fine was sex outside marriage, which is what dominated the docket. So many got caught doing it, or attempting it, that of the 185 known whippings, over 50, the largest single group, were for fornication—sex between unmarried people. Another 50-plus fornication sentences brought offenders the whip-or-fine option. More brought fines only, and several more brought whipping-fine-stocks combinations. Plus, there were 109 cases of the entirely separate crime of "fornication before marriage," for which the guilty—newlyweds whose children arrived suspiciously quickly—were always given the whip-or-fine option. Finally, there were 25 cases of a sexual nature in which no actual sex occurred; "nawty speeches" and unsupervised visits, for instance, were enough to spur inquests.

Bad sex, or no sex, was publicly aired by wives who were dissatisfied enough to prosecute.

Thomas Rolinson, "proven impotent" on the strength of his wife's complaint, was ordered in 1650 to "take counsel of physicians forthwith, follow their advice, and report to court."

Mary White, of Marblehead, charged her husband, Elias, with "insufficiency" in 1661 and sought to be "freed from him" in the high court. Specifically, Elias could not "perform the duty or office of a husband." Marbleheaders William Charles and John Codner deposed that they had asked Elias whether, "when he lay with his wife, if there were any motion in him or no." Elias's confusing answer was yes, "for four or five hours together but when he turned to her it was gone again." Mary had asked him, in the presence of Charles and Codner, "whether or no he had ever made any use of her." He had answered no. Elias confirmed everything, writing, "When I first married, I thought myself sufficient: otherwise I never would have entered into that estate." He wanted to avoid "all further troubles" and added, "I find myself infirmous and not able to perform that office of marriage. What the cause is I know not. I am fully content to be separated if it please this authority." But to Mary's dismay, the judges kept the couple together, advising "a more loving and suitable cohabitation" and suggesting that "all due physical means may be used." Like in the case of "defiling the marriage bed," the record is silent on exactly what "all due physical means" might entail.

In 1673, Thomas Herrick's wife, Hannah, accused him of impotency and got her marriage deemed null and void. She was given her liberty "as if such pretended marriage had never been," and Thomas was to return "whatever he'd gotten of her father or friends in way of [his] marriage portion." Katherine Ellenwood got her marriage annulled in 1682, complaining of her husband Ralph's insufficiency, pleading her youth and insisting she "would rather die than live with this man."

And because husbands also had to be heard, a wife's obligation was also recognized. In 1671, Rachel Clenton had her husband, Lawrence, from whom she was separated, jailed for not paying for her maintenance. Upon his release, Rachel was enjoined "to entertain him as her husband whenever he [visited] upon penalty of being sent to the house of correction." "Entertaining" in Rachel's case implied duty, pleasant or otherwise. In other circumstances the word impugned a woman's morality. Furthermore, wives were to spend their time properly; a Mrs. Magilligon was whipped in 1679 "for absenting herself from her husband, night and day," probably not for the first time.

FORNICATION AND ALL THAT

Preserving the sanctity of marriage was one thing, but there was another reason to forbid extramarital sex. Married fathers tend to support their children; unmarried fathers often don't. Many a Puritan woman was left wondering when, if ever, her man would return. After a birth, if a father couldn't be found or identified, taxpayers paid for raising the child, unless the mother had means, which was rarely the case. If either parent had money or property, it was put up as surety to save taxpayer expense. Many a man proclaimed his innocence but was identified as the reputed father and paid up, whether he was or wasn't. And the standard of proof was pretty low. John Burges had to pay based only on, one, the accusation of Rebecca Outen, who simply said he was "well known," and two, the jury's "vehement suspicion." In another case, Sarah Jones was whipped severely in 1661 on nothing more than "going into a little house that stood apart from another house, where there was no light, during a rainy wedding."

Some fornicators got their fines reduced by marrying. Others, like Isaac and Sara Bailey from Newbury, sought to mollify the court with guilt-laden petitions. "It hath pleased God to leave us to commit folly and to sin against God," the Baileys wrote in their petition to the Ipswich court in 1684,

> and to the dishonor of his name, the scandal of the gospel, and to sin against our own souls, the breach of law, and offence to this honored court and to the great grief of our aged parents, the consideration of which we desire to humbly fall down before God to implore and by his mercy through Jesus Christ for the pardon of our sins and a true sight of the evil of our ways, and we do heartily acknowledge our sin and our fault before God and this honored court, humbly desiring your honors prayer to God for us, and also your honors favor towards us in this cause.

Acceptable opportunities for men and women to be alone, or meet at all, were rare, and a plethora of terms described such latently wicked moments. Couples answered to charges like "insinuating dalliance," "wanton dalliance," "too much familiarity" and, in one instance, simply "being with" each other. Such charges escalated to "unlawful familiarity," "committing folly," "making love" (which meant inappropriate conversation, including calling the wrong people "dear" and "honey"), frequenting each other's company at "unseasonable times" and being together "in a scandalous

Whipping at the Cart's Tayle.

Whippings were sometimes delivered
at a cart's tail and paraded through
town or from town to town.
Illustration by Frank Hazenplug from
Curious Punishments from Days Gone By
(Bibliolife Reproduction Series, 1896)
by Alice Morse Earle.

manner." There was also the odd "incontinency," and at times the more
straightforward "improper relations." Men were accused of "attempting
chastity," "offering abuse," "drawing away affections" and "endeavoring to
draw away affections under pretense of marriage." Women, as previously
noted, were charged with "entertaining."

The county's nascent police state had no shortage of informants, and one
couple was caught with ridiculous ease in their brazen, practically delirious,
infractions. John and Elizabeth Pearce of Ipswich met the whip in 1673
for "uncleanness before marriage." Elizabeth, a widow, had the cheek to

...s at John's house. Not being invisible, she was seen leaving in mornings. John's neighbor Clement Coldam heard about it, chose his moment and looked in their window. He then recruited Anthony Dey and Deacon Stevens as witnesses, and they all "saw enough to warrant a complaint." (Another secret spectator, William Clark, was whipped in 1643 for "spying into the chamber of his master and mistress and reporting what he saw.")

Given the danger involved, it's a wonder liaisons were discussed at all, but for some the pleasure in confessing to forbidden pleasure is irresistible. One day, while out mowing with Samuel Younglove, Edmond Bridges revealed his "undue relations" with not one, but two women. He multiplied his jeopardy exponentially when he also told Simon Stacey about his adventures—*and* complained that Younglove, "the simple fool," had gone and told Thomas Fowlar. Bridges confessed to everything in Ipswich court. One of the women, Mary Quilter, was ordered severely whipped. The other was ordered to watch Bridges' whipping.

Joseph Severans paid a bit less for licentious loquaciousness in 1673. For boasting of his lascivious and unclean practices, he was fined and stood for half an hour at the Hampton meetinghouse door, wearing the words "This person is convicted for speaking words in a boasting manner of his lascivious and unclean practices" on his chest.

FORNICATION BEFORE MARRIAGE

The immutable laws of attraction caused no end of trouble for young people who, despite all odds, found ways to get intimate when the chemistry called for it. Over a hundred cases of fornication before marriage were filed when a birth followed a wedding "too soon." What was usually delivered besides a baby was a guilty verdict, unencumbered by science. But not all such couples were guilty, and it was undoubtedly most vexing to properly abstain, then marry and face the charge anyway. Damned if they did and damned if they didn't, the law-abiding victims of gestation's unpredictability faced the same music as the rule-breakers.

The newlyweds often confessed. Others flattered and fawned and appealed to sympathy. One such, William Barber, wrote, "I humbly entreat the favor of this honored court…[and] hope your honors may be likened unto the kings of Israel of ancient time[s], known to be merciful." Another petitioner submitted her "meek and humble penitence." Thomas Very asked for consideration "to so poor a worm both in respect to estate and guilt." Others just disappeared. And some relied on their good reputations and a savvy midwife, like Sarah White.

White, an experienced and respected midwife, helped one accused couple in 1684, telling the court she had previously delivered a child to a woman who went "but two and thirty weeks" and that the accused woman and her husband were "approved persons both for honesty and godliness." She herself, White said, went "but thirty-five weeks" with her first child. Also, she pointed out, forty years earlier, Martha Rowlyson had been cleared of the charge in Ipswich, having delivered at thirty-five weeks. A records check on marriage dates was made, presumably to everyone's satisfaction, as there is no punishment on record for the midwife's clients.

Those found guilty of fornication before marriage either paid a fine (anywhere from forty shillings to five pounds) or chose between a whipping and a fine. Pregnant women were allowed to give birth before being whipped.

When suspect couples were nowhere near marriageable age, girls were physically examined. Boys were questioned.

What children do with themselves at night under the blankets, impossible to prosecute and therefore beyond law, was simply discouraged. Essex children got two pamphlets, each by famous Puritan minister Cotton Mather. One was *The Pure Nazarite. Advice to a Young Man, Concerning an Impiety and Impurity (Not Easily to Be Spoken of) which Many Young Men Are to Their Perpetual Sorrow, Too Easily Drawn Into.* The other was *Onania: or, the Heinous Sin of Self-pollution, and All Its Frightful Consequences, in Both Sexes, Considered. With Physical and Spiritual Advice to Those Who Have Already Injur'd Themselves by This Abominable Practice.*

ADULTERY AND ALL THAT

Adulterers—a married and an unmarried person together, or two persons married but not to each other—were rarely caught. Only two adultery cases came up in Essex. Whether adulterers were truly rare or just sneakier than fornicators is an open question.

One decidedly unsneaky couple was Philip Darland and Mary Knights. Darland, a Beverly miller, was caught in an orchard engaging in "vile, filthy, and abominably libidinous actions" with the married Knights. He was locked up for a couple of nights and spent an hour on the gallows with a

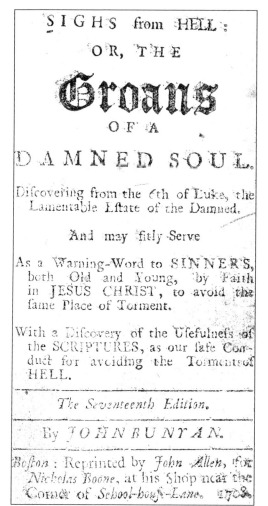

SIGHS from HELL:

OR, THE

Groans

OF A

DAMNED SOUL.

Difcovering from the 6th of Luke, the Lamentable Eftate of the Damned.

And may fitly Serve

As a Warning-Word to SINNERS, both Old and Young, by Faith in JESUS CHRIST, to avoid the fame Place of Torment.

With a Difcovery of the Ufefulnefs of the SCRIPTURES, as our fafe Conduct for avoiding the Torments of HELL.

The Seventeenth Edition.

By JOHN BUNYAN.

Bofton : Reprinted by John Allen, for Nicholas Boone, at his Shop near the Corner of School-houfe-Lane. 1708.

Sighs from Hell: or, the Groans of a Damned Soul epitomizes the Puritan vision of the fate of all sinners. Pamphlet by John Bunyan (1628–1688), reprinted in Boston by John Allen in 1708. *Courtesy American Antiquarian Society.*

rope around his neck. He was then taken down, fastened to the tail of a cart and whipped severely on his bare back while being returned to prison. He stayed in jail until his court costs were paid. Mary renounced her confession, which had convicted Philip, and took her chances at trial. Found guilty, she got the same sentence as he, with "whorish" added for extra vilification.

Another less-than-circumspect couple was John Honiwell, a Marblehead fisherman, and Elizabeth Gilligan, the wife of Alexander Gilligan, also of Marblehead. Their odyssey to and from Black Point (Scarborough, Maine, today) was so infamous that their interrogations were recorded in detail.

On August 10, 1685, after they got home and their story got out, the first attempt to arrest Honiwell failed. Marblehead Constable Vincent Stilson tracked Honiwell to the home of another Marbleheader, John Williams, about seventy-seven. Honiwell had been staying there with Elizabeth. (Elizabeth's husband, like Williams, was elderly.) As the officer climbed the ladder to their bedchamber Honiwell hit him, and "he fell down stunned," according to the complaint, which also said Honiwell was "striking and hurting [the constable] greatly, also pursuing him with a great pole, and swearing by the name of God he would kill him, so that he was forced to defend himself with the black staff." The black staff was the constable's symbol of authority.

Honiwell escaped, but not for long, and meanwhile some damning testimony surfaced. Mary Russell, about fifty, said she had often seen Honiwell "lying in Gilligan's bed" when Elizabeth was in repose at its foot. And Thomas Russell, about thirty-five, said he saw Elizabeth and Honiwell at Williams's house "conversing together with much familiarity."

Elizabeth was arrested September 8 "for absenting herself from her husband and keeping company with Jno. Honiwell." The next day, she was examined in Boston by John Hathorne, a judge at the Court of Assistants:

> *Q. Where have you been these three weeks?*
> *A. I have been to see my relations at the eastward.*
> *Q. Where do your relations live at the eastward?*
> *A. At Black Point.*
> *Q. Have you been at Black Point?*
> *A. No, I was going but dared not because of the Indians, and the English are in their garrisons at the eastward.*

The record notes here that Elizabeth added that she went about three miles past Topsfield and no farther.

> *Q. What did Jno. Honiwell go along with you for?*
> *A. He went to see his relations also, for he hath relations lives at the eastward and it is good to have company with one for it is bad for a woman to go alone through the woods.*
> *Q. Did you not see Jno. Honiwell this morning?*
> *A. Yes, I did see him at a distance in the woods, but did not speak with him.*
> *Q. Why did you leave your husband and go up and down the country and through the woods with another man? Did Jno. Honiwell go with you to the eastward about a fortnight since?*

A. Yes, he went with me so far as I went and that was about three or four miles beyond Topsfield.

Q. Hath not Jno. Honiwell and you agreed to meet tonight?

A. Yes, he desired me to come with him about half an hour within night to a haycock by a small house or cow house in Doctor Knott's land.

Q. Is that true you tell me?

A. Yes, he told me he would be there this evening and desired me to meet him there.

Elizabeth then owned (admitted) that she went with Honiwell all the way to Piscataqua, the region that now separates Maine and New Hampshire, and back. On the day of her questioning, Honiwell was arrested "for profane swearing, abusing the constable and other great crimes," including suspicion of living in adultery with Elizabeth. He appeared before Hathorne on September 10 and acknowledged that

he did sometimes this summer quarter or keep at Jno. Williams' house at Marblehead when Elizabeth Gilligan did lie in the same chamber at the same house, and that he went to the Eastward as far as Black Point with her about a fortnight ago and returned with her, her husband giving his consent.

Honiwell, too, was examined by Hathorne:

Q. How many nights did you lie together in the woods in your travels to the eastward and back again within this fortnight?

A. Three or four nights and no more. The rest of the time we lay in some house or another.

Q. Did not you desire Elizabeth Gilligan to come to you and meet you last night at a haycock by a cow house or hovel in Doctor Knott's land in Marblehead? [People would sometimes use their houses as unlicensed taverns.]

A. Yes.

Q. Is that place where you and Elizabeth Gilligan agreed to meet and lodge last night near any drinking house of anybody's?

A. No, it is not near any dwelling house.

Q. Have [you] *not a wife in England?*

A. Yes, I have, and six children.

Q. How long did you stay at Piscataqua in your journey to the eastward?
A. I was there three or four days.
Q. Did you not steal a turkey when you was at Piscataqua?
*A. Yes, I acknowledge I did and was there fined three or four shillings for it
and paid it and Jonathan Hart of Salem paid twelve shillings of it for me
and Mr. Barefoot was [the] judge that sentenced me and they forgave me
the charges and it was a cock turkey and after that I went to Black Point
and [had] Elizabeth Gilligan with me.*
Q. Why did you steal a cock turkey at Piscataqua?
A. It was for provisions to eat on our journey.

John and Elizabeth went to jail. A couple of weeks later, Jonathan Hart, about forty, traveled to Boston to testify. He had been at Piscataqua at Honiwell's questioning by Squire Barefoot, the deputy governor there. Hart said that Honiwell had with him "a woman said to be old Gilligan's wife of Marblehead" but that Honiwell also said she was *his* wife and that they had been married about five or six weeks.

Elizabeth was convicted of keeping company with Honiwell "both day and night in the fields and woods and in Marblehead, and in their journey to the eastward when they appear to have lived as man and wife." She was severely whipped twenty stripes and told to return to her husband. No further punishment for Honiwell is recorded.

Near-adultery attracted as much attention as the real thing.

One couple carried on in flagrant disregard for the consequences. James Creek answered to "heinous, lascivious and adulterous carriages" with the married Elizabeth Perkins. He had been seen kissing her several times, even on the street, which made Mary Brown "ashamed to be seen in their company." John Brown saw them kissing in the moonlight and tickling each other in the ribs in an orchard and was "so ashamed he went into his own house." The couple was seen at Creek's home after a Sabbath meeting had begun in the afternoon and, on another occasion, "handling linen with their heads close together." Elizabeth would visit his shop and "pull up his hat, look in his face, tickle him and bring him drink, making a great deal more of him than she ever made of her own husband." They didn't help themselves once charges were brought, either. Elizabeth was suddenly nowhere to be found, and James threw fuel on the fire by saying kissing her was "good manners, like other men did." They were obvious but restrained themselves where it counted. They were either abstinent or

Vanity, while not a sin, was implicitly wicked to Puritans. By "P.F.," probably Pompey Fleet, a worker in Thomas Fleet's Boston printing house, circa 1769. From *A Dictionary of Colonial American Printers' Ornaments & Illustrations* (American Antiquarian Society, 1975) by Elizabeth Carroll Reilly. *Courtesy of the American Antiquarian Society.*

cleverer than they seemed and avoided a charge of outright adultery. No punishment is recorded.

Before William and Sarah Row's ill-fated wedding, Sarah was warned by her aunt and uncle not to marry him if she didn't love him. She married anyway and, according to them, was "dissatisfied" and unwilling to accept him as a husband. When William was away on long fishing trips, Sarah enjoyed John Leigh's company. She would sit on Leigh's lap, engaging in "nasty and filthy" discourse. They were seen meeting in a meadow and also at the Browns' house, many times with the outer door shut and the latch pulled in, and sometimes withdrew to an inner room. Finally, Sarah's husband sued Leigh for drawing away Sarah's affections with "insinuating dalliance" and "too much familiarity." Leigh declared his innocence, cleverly pointing out that because Sarah lacked affection for William it was senseless to charge him with stealing it. William won anyway.

Leigh was whipped, and Sarah was imprisoned for a month, both for unlawful familiarity. Furthermore, Sarah wore a sign reading "For my baudish carriage" while in open view of the congregation, and Leigh was bound to good behavior and ordered to stay away from Sarah. He didn't, and neither did she. Two years later, the court was telling Sarah to stay away from Leigh. The record is silent on whether her marriage lasted.

Forever Taboo

Puritans from other counties were executed for bestiality, but none from Essex. The charge did rear its monstrous head in Essex twice, though. Once it was part of a Marblehead indictment but was not followed by a trial. Another time it was a charge proven false at trial (see "Meanies, Creeps and Ne'er-do-Wells").

Rape, or "ravishment," was rarely reported and inconsistently punished. Samuel Guile was convicted of "violently and forcibly" raping Mary Ash of Amesbury in the Haverhill woods on Christmas Day 1674. Guile pleaded not guilty but could not overcome the evidence and was hanged in October 1675. His estate paid six pounds and eighteen shillings for witnesses from Newbury and five pounds in recompense to Mary Ash.

On the other hand, in 1680 William Nelson got only a whipping for raping a girl under the age of ten. The Nelson case was a reminder of the county's most sensational sex case, another in which the perpetrators did not hang. In his journal, Governor Winthrop, who usually covered crimes in a sentence or two, wrote at length about the "very foul sin"[5] prosecuted in 1642. (He is quoted from here to the next endnote.)

Daniel Fairfield, about forty, and his wife, a "lusty young woman," lived and worked at the farm of a Salem magistrate, a Mr. Humphrey. Humphrey "much neglected his children, leaving them among a company of rude servants." Two of Humphrey's daughters, Dorcas and Sarah,

> the eldest not seven, came oft to this Fairfield's house, and were abused by him very often, especially on the Lord's days and lecture days, by agitation and effusion of seed, and after by entering the body of the elder, as it seemed; for upon search she was found to have been forced, and in this course he continued about two years.

Later on, another "lusty young man," John Hudson, an unmarried servant of Humphrey's who sometimes worked on the farm, got the older girl, then about eight, to come to bed with him and abused her "many times so as she was grown capable of man's fellowship and took pleasure in it." (There is no mention of the girls' mother in either Winthrop's journal or the record, so they likely didn't have one.)

When Humphrey went to England, the girls went to Lynn to live with the carpenter Jenkin Davis and his pregnant wife, who was temporarily uninterested in sex. Davis, "hurried by the strength of his lust," tried to abuse the older girl, then about nine, but was "constantly denied any entrance of her body."

Nothing was known about any of this until the abused girl told an older, newly married sister, who sounded the alarm. Upon examination, the younger girl gave details of her experiences with not only the three men but also with two of her brothers, who were so young "they could not use any semination, and so were referred to private correction."

"Thus was this family secretly polluted," Winthrop wrote.

The men confessed to everything but entrance to the girl's body, and so the debate began—across Massachusetts and Connecticut, for months—about whether it was sodomy, rape or something else. The girl had consented, but the judges decided it was rape because she was "unripe" and "not of understanding fit to give consent."

It was ultimately agreed, based on the girl's examination, and despite denials by her and the men, that she had been completely violated and that the men should die. But neither God's law nor Puritan law provided *that* sentence for *that* crime at *that* time, so debate continued. Finally, Fairfield was convicted of grossly immoral conduct and threatened with execution should he ever do it again. They severely whipped him in Boston and slit one nostril "as high as may well be." They whipped him again in Salem, where they slit his other nostril and seared it (so natural healing would not hide the disfigurement). Between whippings, he was kept in Boston "til he be fit" for his Salem appearance. Davis and Hudson were whipped at Boston and Lynn, and Davis had to wear a halter. The men received their punishments "very patiently, without any striving or complaining though they had near forty stripes." Humphrey received £100 in fines, £40 each from Fairfield and Davis and £20 from Hudson.

Fairfield was confined to Boston Neck, departure from which, either by land or beyond the low-water mark, would put him to death. Further, he was "to wear a hempen rope about his neck, the end of it hanging out two foot at least, and so often as he be found abroad without it, he shall be whipped, and if he shall at any time hereafter attempt to abuse any person as formerly, he shall be put to death."[6]

Fairfield's sainted wife pleaded for years that his sentence be commuted, and finally, in 1652, the court let the rope come off:

> *However, there was little chance for the disfigured Fairfield to live down his disgrace. Twice he petitioned for leave to get away from the colony altogether and in 1656 he was granted liberty to sail to England provided, should he ever return, he would go back to prison.*[7]

Incest was another rarely uncovered taboo. John Southwick's son and daughter were fined for uncleanness in Salem in 1672, which was sensational but not as sensational as the outright charge of incest brought against Nicholas Manning and his sisters in Ipswich in 1680.

Manning quarreled with his wife, Elizabeth—so much so that she, in fear of her life, went to stay with a daughter. When her husband sent her no support, she petitioned the Ipswich selectmen for maintenance. Meanwhile, rumors were spreading, and Manning heard that the charge against him was imminent.

The night before he was accused, Elizabeth explained afterward, Manning wanted her back home. She, "knowing nothing, was overcome by his fair speeches and went home with him that night," only later "finding his intent was to make use of me but as a cloak."

Manning was found guilty of incestuous practices with his sisters, Anstis Manning and Margaret Palfree, on the strength of testimony (not provided) from five witnesses. The sisters' sentences—to be stripped and whipped—were remitted with a five-pound fine. They did, however, spend the next lecture day in Salem in the open middle alley of the meetinghouse wearing paper hats that spelled out their crime.

Manning avoided trial by running off, never to be seen again. He continued to deny his wife financial support, and she was granted a divorce and his estate. In the end, Elizabeth Manning probably wanted as little to do with her husband as he did with her. Years later—rather anticlimactically—he wrote to "utterly" renounce her and declare he "will not own her for his wife or have anything to do with her."

Manning left Essex but lives on in the record, as do many others whom the righteous preferred to avoid.

Creeps, Meanies and Ne'er-do-wells

First prize in the Essex creep parade goes to Robert Crose Jr. for sacrilege, or, as the court put it, the "barbarous and inhuman act of digging up the grave of the Sagamore of Agawam."

Crose did not stop at unearthing the Indian's bones. He hoisted the skull on a pole and used it as a prop for the profoundly unfunny joke of intending to give it to his wife to use as a grease pot. Then he carried it into Ipswich and paraded it through the streets.

The sagamore, or chief, was Masconomet, who had sold large portions of Essex to the settlers. One of the region's best-known Indians, then and now, he died in 1658 and was buried with his gun, tomahawk and other tools of the hunt. Crose dug him up nine years later. John Gidding was plowing a nearby field and, when shown the skull, said it had "something like brains or jelly in it." When Gidding asked for it to be taken away, they—Crose and his accomplice, John Andrews Jr.—refused.

Indians were not generally held in high esteem by Puritans. Some considered them subhuman. But Crose's stunt was so broadly offensive he was imprisoned until the next lecture day, when he went in the stocks for an hour and then returned to prison until a fine of over six pounds—enough for several acres—was paid. He also had to rebury the skull and what other bones could be found and build a two-foot-high pile of stones over the new grave. Andrews had to help and make a public acknowledgement of his wrongdoing.

Masconomet's grave is located today atop Sagamore Hill in Hamilton, graced at all times with offerings of spirit and tokens of reverence.

Grave site of Masconomet on Sagamore Hill in Hamilton, festooned with offerings as always. *Author photo.*

Crose's thoughtless disregard for the sanctity of life and death was complemented by equally senseless and pointless attacks on animals by others.

Joseph Daliver was jailed until he paid ten pounds to the owners of the horses he shot dead on Marblehead common. In twisted yet unassailable logic, Daliver said he wished all horses were killed because they ate all the cows' feed. John Chub paid five pounds to Reynold Foster (under threat of a whipping) for spearing Foster's horse, which was found bloody and had been seen lying in the snow most of the day, with a pitchfork nearby. Chub's explanation went undocumented. George Farough was charged with stealing six hogs and shoats, removing a property landmark and "cruelty in drowning a mare." He was disenfranchised and would have been whipped but for his petition of humiliation. Exactly how he drowned the mare is unexplained. (One might presume she was asked to carry all his booty through a body of water at once.) A horse sold for six pounds, or twelve, or more.

Another man had to justify shooting a tamed deer, which had been painstakingly marked as such with a red collar around its neck.

Nancy and Simon Hoar got six lashes each from the Beverly constable for beating a cow to death. The cow, one of several that were attacked, belonged to John Hale, pastor of the Beverly church. The Hoars were "vengeful" against Hale, who also had his hay stolen and the walls of his house knocked on at night when his family was inside without him. Nancy Hoar was seen "with a great stick in her hands" beating the cows, while her husband and "the Johnson boys" kept them within her reach with clubs. William Dodge Sr., called to assist Hale, said the cow "could not rise without help," and later, "when her skin was off, she was very black upon the ribs."

Richard Shatswell's ox suffered the same fate. Shatswell sued William Delow "for cruelty in beating his ox, whereby he is much diminished, the ox being dead." The ox, borrowed to haul wood, was "so beaten that the hair was off"—an accomplishment perhaps not as painstaking as collaring a deer but especially time-consuming in its own way.

On a lighter, prankish note, Thomas and John Manning were fined for "putting a calf in the chimney of Mark Quilter," who was fined, in turn, for excessive drinking. The calf presumably survived.

Thefts and abuses of livestock were just one aspect of crime down on the farm. (Down at the docks, drunken fishermen got distracted and let the catch spoil.) Field hands made sheaves of wheat look larger and fuller than they really were. Farmers were constantly cutting each other's hay, pulling down each other's fences, relocating boundary stakes and turning hungry swine into each other's corn with devastating results. The sun came up and the sun went down, and agricultural war was waged over hill and dale.

BOORISH LOUTS, CHURLISH CADS AND OTHER HOPELESS ROMANTICS

Women have always endured men's crude advances, and life in old Essex left them particularly isolated and unprotected, what with their husbands out farming, fishing, traveling and hunting. Then as now they were all targets in the eyes of the ill-intentioned—be they married, unmarried or widowed. Puritan widows were often young; among them were many considered as such whenever their husbands, gone away to sea two or three years running, showed up missing.

In a world without matches, one common ruse was to request a light for a pipe from a woman's hearth. It was a common enough courtesy. But when

Reconstructed stocks and pillory at the Whipple House in Ipswich, circa 1677. *Author photo.*

the smoker had wicked intentions, there were four options: call for help, get behind a locked door, run or fight.

One character, a man named Morrin, took a shine to the wife of James Waters. He visited her and her husband at their house, and when James went out for cider, Morrin assaulted her. Nothing more came of it, but he returned another day and knocked on her door. Getting no answer, he looked in the window and asked her for a light. She conceded on the condition that he be civil, but when he walked in, as she later testified, "he came directly at me." As she ran out, Morrin told her "if he had not his will of me now, the next time he met me he would be the death of me." Morrin got the whip-or-fine option for "offering abuse."

Giving a man directions could get dicey, too. George Dymond asked Mary Caley for directions one night and, having lured her out into the dark, made his move. He got the same sentence as Morrin.

Other men just walked in, or broke in, or caught women out in the barn. John Smith forced open an outer bolted door and two inner latched doors to get to John Glover's wife one night. He was severely whipped for the break-in and for uncivil carriages to her. ("Carriage" meant a person's overall behavior, conduct, deportment and manners.) Seven years later, in 1672, Smith was whipped again for "several abusive and uncivil carriages" toward another woman, Elizabeth Goodell.

In 1670, an Indian called Nimrod (the biblical term for "mighty hunter") walked in—without knocking—on Edmund James's wife with three other Indians, carrying guns and hatchets. The Indians sat by the fire and asked if she had a husband. Told yes, they asked where. Told nearby, they said she was lying and started looking for food. When Nimrod spoke again, in a "baudy" way, she sat with her back to him, knitting. The Indians laughed and left, but the next morning admitted to entering and attempting abuse. Nimrod and another Indian served twenty days.

Mary Roffe was a magnet for the wrong type. Poor and young, and with her husband away, she told the court she had arranged for another couple's daughter "to lie with me" until her husband returned. But the lying-in girl had to work and eat at her own house, where she lived with her father, so Mary had to sometimes visit there, which was where Henry Greenland had come to live. Greenland, a doctor, "catched me by the apron and broke my apron strings, and I gave way to save my apron and he caught me by the arm and pulled me," Mary testified in 1663. Greenland said he'd let her go if Mr. Emery (the lying-in girl's father) said it was uncivil, but Mr. Emery just laughed.

"With striving I got from him," Mary said, and everyone ate. But after supper, there was "a great deal of rude and uncivil discourse," and liquor was forced down her throat.

Greenland often "enticed her to the act of uncleanness" and once came into her bed at night. He also offered to take her to Jamaica or Nevis, where, he said, a man could have more than one wife. He was convicted of soliciting her to adultery, jailed and offered the choice of a whipping or a hefty thirty-pound fine. But Mary, too, was fined: her claim that Emery had brought Greenland to her without her knowledge lost out to their assertion that she had invited them.

Another medical man, Richard Cordin, caught Mary in her mother's stable. Acting as physician to her mother, Cordin put the older woman to sleep with a potion, then asked Mary to "show him where her horse was." At first she objected, but not wanting to cross the good doctor, she went with him into the stable. Once inside, he knocked the candle out of her hand. When she cried out, he warned her not to tell of it, which of course she did. Cordin got the option of a whipping or a twenty-pound fine. He got out of jail by promising to depart the court's jurisdiction within a week.

SPITFIRES AND HELLCATS

Obviously, seventeenth-century women could ill afford to be tender flowers. Mrs. Philip Logee was in bed when "Joseph, William Trask's Indian," came in and woke her by lying down next to her. Thinking it was her husband home from sea, she spoke to him. Getting no answer, she looked closer in the moonlight and saw it was someone else. The spunky Mrs. Logee took the Indian "by the hair and beat him with her fist but he got away out the window, [the] door being locked." She also called to John King, a young lodger, to "get someone and kill him."

Other women were tougher yet, and meaner.

Mary Oliver relished attacks on authority and seemed indifferent to whippings. Unique in the record's cast of unsavory characters, she was twice ordered out of the colony and twice flouted that order by returning. Nothing stilled her acerbic tongue in her dozen court appearances over twenty years' time.

Oliver first appears in the record in 1639, about to be escorted by two constables to an indefinite stay in Boston prison for her verbal abuse (unfortunately not documented) of some newcomers upon their arrival in Salem. A twenty-pound bond ensuring her appearance at the next Boston court delayed that trip, but she was soon back to be admonished for condemning the ordinance of God and speaking other "unseemly passages." She was back again to be whipped for saying someone who should have been vindicated by the court had been mistreated instead.

She took her second whipping with a cleft stick on her tongue for her blasphemous comment that all ministers in the country were "bloodthirsty." When she was being sentenced, she audaciously told the judges her blood was "too thin for them to draw out."

Oliver was fined and set in the stocks for other things, like abusing Captain Hathorne, working on the Sabbath and telling the court, "You in New England are thieves and robbers." At one point, refusing to post a bond to ensure better behavior, she did see the inside of the Boston jail.

Robert Gutch said Oliver came to his house one day in 1647, curiously being "in such gladness of spirit" that he could not understand it, telling people to "lift up your heads, your redemption draweth nigh." Gladness mixed with madness perhaps. When Gutch asked if she remembered this passage: "That there were some whose necks had iron sinews and brows of brass," she told him "she did hope to live to tear my flesh in pieces and all such as I were."

The Pillory.

Pilloried criminals had no defense against whatever was thrown at them. Illustration by Frank Hazenplug, from *Curious Punishments from Days Gone By* (Bibliolife Reproduction Series, 1896) by Alice Morse Earle.

In 1648, Mary won ten shillings in damages from constable John Robinson for false imprisonment. Robinson had seized her "in a violent manner" and thrown her straight into the stocks. Also that year she was ordered, under the threat of a twenty-pound fine, to go back to England in the next ship. That she may have done, but she was back in court a year later for stealing goats. Another time, calling the governor "unjust, corrupt, and a wretch" for making her pay for the goats "when there was no proof in the world of it" got her close to another whipping. It was respited on the condition that, again, she leave or, as the court put it, "go into the bay with Joseph Hardy this day or when he goeth next into the bay with his vessel." Her fine was remitted, too, on the condition that she use the money to pay for "transporting herself and children out of this jurisdiction within three weeks."

She probably obeyed, but was back in court in 1661 with her husband, Thomas, for fighting. They were given the choice of a fine or ten stripes each. A neighbor deposed that when the couple asked him to privately referee their spats, she showed up bruised and bloody. Yet, in all likelihood, unbowed.

Sarah Stickney, a widow with four children, was also not to be trifled with. When she was having trouble with Samuel Lowell, a sailor who had been breaking into her house at late hours in 1679, she asked her brother to stay with her. He did and "laid hands" on Lowell one night between two and three in the morning. Lowell got away but lost a shoe in the struggle, which was good evidence. He asked Sarah's brother to say nothing about it, but the detail came out in court anyway. But Sarah's character was put into question by John Mighill. Mighill said Sarah had been at his house just after her husband died, with Lowell and some other seamen, "very jocund and merry, sitting in their laps." It was wrong for her to "carry herself so lightly so soon after her husband's death," Mighill thought. Sarah was fined, and Lowell was released in his father's custody.

One day sometime afterward, John March, riding past Sarah's house in a cart with Lowell and John Atkinson Jr., called to her and said, "Here is Sam Lowell, what have you to say to him?"

"You rogue," she replied, "yonder is your child under the tree, go take it up and see it." To which Lowell replied it was none of his.

In 1681, Sarah was convicted of fornication in Newbury, an easy prosecution, she being a widow and "having birthed a child January last." In 1682, she brought the child into court and fingered Atkinson as the father. Atkinson, it was said, had visited the child, picking it up and kissing it. He had spurred Sarah into legal action by reneging on his promise of support, she said. Before the case was heard, Atkinson and his wife were visiting at Jonathan Haynes's house when Sarah walked in and asked if he was going to deny his child. Atkinson's wife called Stickney an "impudent baud." Stickney let loose with such "reviling speeches" she was told to leave. When she wouldn't, Atkinson's wife clapped her hand in Stickney's face. Not to be outdone, Stickney spat at hers.

Atkinson paid.

ROGUES, KNAVES AND RASCALS

Some men, instead of bringing grief to animals and women, kept it mainly among themselves. Ruben Guppy, Giles Corey, Dr. Richard Knott and John Godfrey were a few of them.

Ruben Guppy's misadventures were bringing him in front of judges right into his eighties, when he was fined for selling strong drink without a license, not for the first time; his residence once topped the list of places to check for illegal, private "tippling houses."

As a young man in 1640, Guppy was caught running away from his pregnant wife and for stealing, lying and swearing. He had been found with stolen axes and seen with a hen in his britches. He was blasphemous, too. When tithingmen (church police) Samuel and Robert Fuller visited, Ruben told them he did not go to meeting and that the parings of his nails were as acceptable to God as the day of thanksgiving. That got him severely whipped. He had a habit of stealing fences, too, and once disobeyed the constable by refusing to participate in a hue and cry. ("Hue and cry" is from

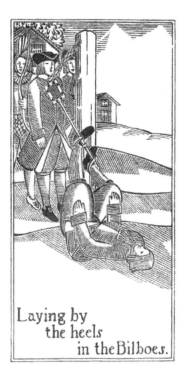

Laying by the heels in the Bilboes.

The bilboes were a portable substitute for the stocks. Illustration by Frank Hazenplug, from *Curious Punishments from Days Gone By* (Bibliolife Reproduction Series, 1896) by Alice Morse Earle.

the Latin *hutesim et clamor*, or "horn and shouting," and everyone was obliged to assist constables in the chase after suspects when so ordered.)

An unspecified defamation charge in 1648 presented Guppy with the choice of a fine or time in the stocks. In 1674, he was charged with saying that Mr. Higgenson, the minister, was complaining about his lack of food when in fact he had plenty. But Guppy revealed his true wickedness in 1657 at the Court of Assistants in Boston, where he had been sent by the Salem court to prosecute his charge of bestiality against Richard Pitfold. It took three weeks of trial, but the charge was deemed false and Pitfold was acquitted.

"Had it been true," wrote the high court, the charge would have endangered Pitfold's life. Guppy paid all costs and was whipped "not exceeding twenty stripes." Had the law against bearing false witness in a capital case been fully enforced, he would have been executed.

Giles Corey was the only person in the New World executed by pressing, or *peine forte et dure*, "hard and forceful punishment"—the death he met as an alleged witch. In the process he achieved fame by calling for "more weight!" Pressing was considered the worst form of execution, as it could take days and was sometimes carried out with a sharp stone under the victim's back. It had been abolished in the colony, but such things meant little during the Salem witch hysteria. Corey secured a place in history, but that doesn't mean he was particularly principled.

Some of Corey's offenses included sleeping on watch (and once having his weapon stolen from him while doing so), fetching a canoe load of wood during watch (and lying about it in court) and stealing foodstuffs, tobacco, knives and "several small things, some of which he confessed and some proved."

In 1650, John Kiching threw "stinking water" on him, probably a slops bucket and probably for good reason. As Corey described it, Kiching then

> *fell upon me and caught me by the throat...and held me so long til he had almost stopped my breath. I said, this is not good jesting, and John Kiching replied, this is nothing, I do owe you more than this of old: this is not half of that which you shall have afterwards.*

Corey got away briefly but was caught again and beaten bloody.

But Corey could dish it out, too, and one man *he* beat died. Brought to court on "suspicion of abusing the body of Jacob Goodell," Corey had been seen "unreasonably" hitting Goodell with a stick "about an inch through and…with the great end…struck him nearly a hundred blows," a witness said. The sight so aggrieved the witness that he told Corey he would knock him down if he didn't stop. Goodell, on his deathbed, said Corey's son-in-law, John Parker, had joined in the attack. Corey was fined an undisclosed sum.

There was much testimony pro and con over the years about Corey and his wife, Mary, who herself received fines for cursing, swearing, abusive speeches and drunkenness. (A charge of beating a servant didn't stick to her because it could not be proven to have happened within a year, the statute of limitations for many crimes.) When Mary accused Martha Bates of milking the Coreys' cows as they came out of the woods by the Bateses' door, the Coreys were successfully sued for defamation.

John Proctor was another Corey enemy. Proctor, immortalized in Arthur Miller's *The Crucible*, was, like Corey, destined to die a witch's death. Before that, however, Proctor was fined for selling cider and "strong water" to the Indians in part on Corey's testimony, and Corey was suspected of setting Proctor's house on fire. The arson charge was dismissed due to lack of evidence: Corey said he was home all that night. Corey then sued Proctor for defaming him with the arson charge. During *that* trial, two deponents swore Corey had threatened to burn *another* man's orchard fence. One deponent swore Corey had threatened several times to turn horses onto his grounds, had stolen from him and was "a very quarrelsome and contentious bad neighbor."

The belief used to be that Corey was crushed to death for not answering the witchcraft charge. Refusals to answer a charge—to plead either guilty or innocent—were common in England because they allowed the heirs of the accused to inherit the accused's property. Pleading guilty *and* being executed, on the other hand, transferred the accused's property to the Crown. It was further believed that Corey was gaming the system to ensure his children's inheritance by not pleading. But according to *The Case of Giles Corey*,[8] he *did* plead guilty, knowing that forfeitures of estates generated by refusals to plea did not apply in witchcraft cases. What he refused to answer was the *next* standard question, the one about how he wanted to be tried.

The custom was to answer that question with "by God and my country," implying a desire for judgment by God and by a jury, or men of the country. By choosing neither, Corey wordlessly defined his trial as a sham. He simply refused to participate, using his silent expression of disdain and contempt to end his trial before it began.

Corey may have also wanted to speed the end. He was in his eighties. He had been in prison for some time. His wife was in jail and likely to join him and all the other accused witches in death, as none had been found innocent. (None in Salem ever was.) His children's inheritance was secured. But when all was unsaid and done, the man who refused to speak had to endure the final, gruesome irony of being *unable* to speak if he wanted to. As he lay dying, the weight forced Corey's tongue out of his mouth. According to Robert Calef, a Boston merchant who witnessed much of the hysteria, "the sheriff with his cane forced it in again."[9]

Dr. Richard Knott owned several vessels and employed many fishermen. He also sold them room and board in his Marblehead home and sometimes

Letters signifying specific crimes were branded into the back, hand, thumb and forehead. Illustration by Frank Hazenplug, from *Curious Punishments from Days Gone By* (Bibliolife Reproduction Series, 1896) by Alice Morse Earle.

assumed their debts. But he had a mean, spiteful streak. That, and his intolerance for disobedience, made him a hard man to work for. Two of his fishermen tried to quit, much to their chagrin.

William Jerman, who owed a third man ten pounds, was, he said, "enticed" to let Knott assume his debt. When Jerman thought his catches had paid Knott off, Knott disagreed, claiming Jerman "had no true account of the weight of the fish." When Knott learned that Jerman was planning to fish for someone else, he said "he would make him know he was his servant." Knott had him imprisoned as a debtor in "a bitter cold" December of 1679.

Knott lorded it over another fisherman the same way in 1682, when Job Tookey decided to stand up to him. Tookey had contracted in February to fish for Knott, for board and wages for seven months. One day, Tookey said he'd done enough and would no longer work for Knott. His contract, Tookey said, was for local fishing, not a long trip "southward for corn" that Knott wanted him to make. When he told Knott he wouldn't go on such a long voyage without a third hand, Knott punched him in the face and beat him with a stick.

The next day, the underhanded Knott suggested that Tookey seek work in Salem on another boat and have his new employer pay the seven pounds in silver. (Tookey had worked it down from nine.) But that night back at Knott's house, Knott reversed himself and asked Tookey if he would fish again for *him* instead. Tookey would not and said he hoped Knott "would be as good as his promise, which had been made in the presence of others, that he would not put me into any of his shallops unless I was willing."

After a couple of days, having been laid low with a pain in his side (perhaps from his beating), Tookey went to Salem to find a new job. But the doctor was a step ahead of him. Tookey found a constable instead—and an attachment for full payment of his debt. Tookey

> begged of [Knott] *humbly not to send me to prison for I told him I could not pay him his engagements in prison, and likewise told him I would willingly serve him in his ketch to go to the southward for corn, or else go fishing in one of his shallops, but the more I begged of him the more he cursed and swore,* [saying] *I should go to jail though I rotted there.*

Into prison he went, and out of prison came a stream of letters. He wrote Knott on March 24, saying that unless released, "I shall undoubtedly be starved with the cold, and shall willingly serve you or yours either by night or by day as far as I can possible."

Another letter again sought release "from this dismal wretched place" and offered to do what the doctor had asked, but Knott's taste for cruelty was not so easily satisfied. In fact, his appetite grew.

On March 30, Knott went to the jail, but only to scold the keeper, Goodman Felton, which he did so thoroughly Felton told Tookey he would "better suffer imprisonment [himself] than go to sea with such a man."

In mid-May, Tookey was encouraged to hear that Knott was planning another visit to the jail and again hoped for release from that "sad, dolesome stinking place." But his hopes were dashed when he heard Knott planned to keep him there until his court appearance, then get an execution against him and sell him to a Virginia planter. That would add, Tookey wrote, "affliction to affliction." And so Tookey wrote the court, beseeching "your Honors [to] take notice of this Doctor Knott's actings." Then, back to Knott, he wrote he was daily "being almost poisoned with the stink of my own dung and the stink of the prison, having never had so much as a minute's time to take the air."

On June 5, Knott appeared at Tookey's prison window for a bit of taunting, and a boy confirmed for him afterward that Knott indeed planned to sell him to Virginia or Barbados.

"I beseech your Honors to take notice and consider this Doctor Knott's inveterate spirit," Tookey's next letter to the court said. Then he wrote Knott again, asking for mercy, clothes, a Bible and some books.

In a June 16 letter to the court, Tookey told how Knott had come to the jail yet again. Knott had called Tookey by name, "whereupon I looked out of the prison window and saw him scrape with his stick on the ground."

"Job," Knott said, "do you know what this means?"

Tookey answered that he did not.

"Oh, Sirrah," Knott replied, "you are like to learn how in Virginia."

The doctor was showing Tookey his future, that of a laborer working the soil.

The cause of Tookey's debt, and all his trouble, was then revealed and makes his tale all the more tragic. He had severed the sinews in his right hand, which had lamed him for over six months and put him in the debt of a different doctor for his cure and convalescence. Dr. Knott had assumed the debt Tookey owed to the first doctor, the one who treated him.

"The debt which Dr. Knott says he has engaged to pay on my behalf I did not owe through any extravagance," Tookey wrote the judges. "I might have paid Mr. [Dr.] Wentworth of Piscataqua…but have been maliciously

The branks silenced scolds and gossips. A "curb plate," sometimes spiked, pressed down on the tongue. Illustration by Frank Hazenplug, from *Curious Punishments from Days Gone By* (Bibliolife Reproduction Series, 1896) by Alice Morse Earle.

debarred from it and kept here by a wretched man falsely." Having languished in prison so long, he added, he had less than half the strength he'd had going in "and will never get back my lost time."

Essex debtors in the business class had their own scourge—the infamous John Godfrey, a ruthless, litigious, bottom-feeding opportunist; a wheeler-dealer, loan shark, thief and witness intimidator who made a career of exploiting people who needed money.

The courtroom was Godfrey's second home. He appeared nearly a hundred times in the twenty-six years between 1649 and 1675 as complainant, defendant and a few times acting as an attorney for others. He earned enough enmity through spite and his abrasive style to have to defend himself against a concerted effort to get him hanged as a witch (see "In the Murderers' Playground"), but he seemed to have friends in high places. Despite damning testimony from a dozen enemies, he was merely "rendered suspicious" of witchcraft in Ipswich and then, in Boston, found "suspiciously guilty of witchcraft, but not legally guilty." Eleven pages of depositions against him show how badly his enemies wanted him dead. Godfrey uniquely benefited by other decisions, too: four times the court simply "did not accept" verdicts that went against him, including one for debt, one for unjust molestation and another for slander. No one else in the record received such high-handed—and questionable—consideration from the powers that be.

Godfrey was a moving target, living as if in fear of retribution, avoiding exposure to vandalism, arson, liens and attachments by never holding any real property for long. He had money but apparently did not own a house. He always gave his address as someone else's house, and his court appearances identify him variously as a resident of Salem, Andover and Newbury. His record is a long list of contests over convoluted agreements, many involving multiple assumptions of debt by various individuals, with Godfrey always somewhere in the middle, parasitically turning a profit.

People beholden to Godfrey via mortgages and bonds paid promptly or suffered the consequences. He was seen "in a rage" and "in a great passion" over money owed him and would leave discussions "without answering." One debtor, referring to a payment he made to Godfrey in corn, said, "I'd rather it were in a heap on the street and all the town hogs eat it than he should keep it in his hands." Another dared not testify because Godfrey "might take away all that he had." A 1668 arrest warrant sought the outspoken ship's carpenter Thomas Wells for allegedly reproaching the Ipswich court by saying, "Old Bradstreet was a worse usurer than Godfrey." Wells hastily denied, in writing, that he had ever "compared the honored magistrates to Godfrey."

John Singletary once offered him a piece of land as payment, but Godfrey would not grant him a general acquitance as part of their settlement. Singletary sued and got an acquitance "from the beginning of the world to February 18, last." Unfazed, Godfrey sued Singletary for debt again as if nothing had happened, and lost again. Singletary then mistakenly asked out loud, "Is this witch on this side [of the] Boston gallows yet?" Godfrey and others heard it, and Singletary was convicted of slander and defamation before long.

Sometimes Godfrey would bring a debtor to court just to have a large bill of costs abated by a few shillings. Sometimes he would refuse payment in the form it was offered. Other times he wouldn't show up to take payment, which burdened the debtor with the cost and frustration of a pointless and futile delivery. One debtor offered cattle and told Godfrey he could choose his own appraisers. Godfrey refused "and would have had them at his own price."

When Richard Ormsbee filed a case against him but didn't prosecute, Godfrey sued for unjust molestation. Ormsbee was one of three sued by Godfrey for failure to prosecute that year, 1661. Five years later, Godfrey charged John Atkinson for failing to prosecute and, in another case, for beating and abusing him while he was Atkinson's prisoner. William Randall supported Godfrey in that case, testifying that Atkinson had taken him "roughly." During the arrest, when asked what his authority was, Atkinson had pointed to his black staff. When Atkinson got the prisoner Godfrey to Goodman Moody, the full-fledged constable, Moody said he would not be responsible; he reminded Atkinson that when he let him take the staff, "he wished to have nothing to do with Godfrey."

Godfrey prosecuted Abraham Whittaker in 1671 for taking a false oath against him and, unsatisfied with the judgment, took three cows out of Whittaker's yard in Haverhill. Whittaker raised a hue and cry, reclaimed the cows and had Godfrey arrested. Godfrey claimed he was detained under pretense and that the hue and cry, and the return of the cows to Whittaker, should not have been done without replevin (a court writ).

The ducking stool, or chair, punished many wicked types, including prostitutes and dishonest tradesmen. Illustration by Frank Hazenplug, from *Curious Punishments from Days Gone By* (Bibliolife Reproduction Series, 1896) by Alice Morse Earle.

Whittaker attempted revenge later, as a marshal's deputy, when he refused to levy two executions Godfrey wanted served and was promptly sued for his refusal.

Mathias Button was on Godfrey's enemies list, too. Button's wife, Elizabeth, had testified to Godfrey's alleged witchcraft. When Button's house burned down, resulting in Elizabeth's death, Button sued Godfrey for its "willful firing." Found guilty, Godfrey got a whopping £238 fine and, as a flight risk, also posted a £100 bond. (For perspective, a jewel in the estate of Massachusetts governor John Endicott, consisting of a house, acreage and orchards, was valued at £550.) Abiel Somerby testified that some people in Salisbury would have been bound on Godfrey's behalf had the judge not said that even if Godfrey went to the farthest part of New England, he would have him brought back in chains or irons. James Ordway backed Somerby up, saying he himself had intended to be bound for Godfrey but didn't because "the matter was made so odious by the court."

Godfrey, true to form, turned around and sued Button, but that backfired. He lost and in the process set the stage for another conviction.

Abraham and Elizabeth Whittaker testified that "many times in the past summer John Godfrey tried to persuade them with many fawning speeches to make oath for them against Button of Haverhill." Godfrey had asked them to say that Button had lied, had told people his own children had caused the fire. For their cooperation, he offered the Whittakers forty pounds and a promise to "never sue them anymore." Godfrey also offered the pregnant Elizabeth "whatever she might want in connection with the coming child." Others testified that they had heard Goody Whittaker say Godfrey had offered her wool and cash for her time as a witness for him. The result was, later that year (1669), Godfrey was fined another £100 in Salisbury for his "wicked and most pernicious subborning [of] witnesses" and for the "perverting of justice" both by himself and by instigating others, "sometimes by hindering persons from giving evidence and sometimes to give false evidence."

His sentence included an hour in the pillory wearing a sign saying, "John Godfrey for subborning witnesses." He was also "utterly disabled from giving evidence in any case hereafter unless he be restored by authority." He was to be imprisoned after being pilloried, but James Orday and Robert Beadle approached Godfrey upon his release from the pillory and offered him his liberty if he would release three men—Edward Phillips, Thomas Linsford and Button—from their debts to him.

"Godfrey," they said, "being afraid of the prison, having had experience with the miserable place, agreed to anything."

At other times, Godfrey faced charges of lying, drunkenness, cursing, fighting, smoking in the streets and traveling on the Sabbath. He was convicted of battery after "pummeling" Robert Purnell in the street after Purnell dared tell him, two or three times, to pay what Godfrey owed *him*. In 1667, Godfrey was convicted of stealing seven beaver skins, a beaver cap "and other things" from a warehouse belonging to Stephen Sergeant. He was told to pay Sergeant treble damages, plus five pounds to the county, or be whipped fifteen stripes. He appealed instead, even though it meant returning to prison for want of security. Godfrey then pleaded with Robert Lord, "the best friend he had," to act as his attorney. Lord obliged—and then had to sue to get paid.

Even death didn't stop Godfrey from plaguing people with legal wrangling. In 1677, a written testament of his was used to invalidate a deed. In it, he claimed to have been drunk when he signed the deed.

Godfrey was a bully in business and law, the worst of his era. Physical bullies inspire a different kind of fear and loathing, and their malevolence was not visited only upon adults.

Bruisers, Biters and Brats

When "spare the rod and spoil the child" and "better whipped than damned" were words to live by, there weren't any complaints of child abuse. Not in families, anyway. For Puritan children, corporal punishment was part of growing up; it just happened, like the weather. But it was no more acceptable in seventeenth-century Essex than it is today for someone outside the family to hit a child—except the schoolmaster. All children have mischief in them, and schoolmasters were expected to maintain order and discipline, with "full power to punish any and all scholars."[10]

But Samuel Hall of Salisbury was not a schoolmaster and was fined twenty-five shillings for beating Phoebe Driver, who was about eight, in 1643. Several Haverhill children were so abused by Benjamin Longe that he got six stripes in 1652. That same year, Joseph Langton of Marblehead answered to his "evil usage of a little child of his wife" (not his). To quiet the child, Langton whipped it twice with "a sticky rod, the small branches being worn off." One deponent said the child had to lie in a straw bed with "a piece of sailcloth or some such material in the cradle" and could not remember whether it had a pillow for its head. The child was sent to its grandparents. In Topsfield, Mary Hadley complained that Zacheous Curtis had whipped her "with a rod with my feet under his arms and my head on the ground, and then made me pull off my coats and whipped me again." Curtis was himself whipped for that.

Grownups could get a wink and a nod, though, if there was some reason behind their lack of restraint. Thomas Maule was merely admonished for hitting George Dean's children; they had cut down his apple trees.

Whether or not the children of the widower John Blaine were beaten is unknown, and almost beside the point: their main cross to bear was egregious neglect. While quite young, they inherited a farm from their grandfather, Daniel King, who disliked his son-in-law. That made Blaine the custodial parent of minors yet to come into their inheritance.

The Blaine place didn't produce much, just what the woodlot made, plus rents from a team and from tenants Mark and Elizabeth Graves. Blaine drank what proceeds there were. There was only one cow, somehow appropriate for someone trying to milk a farm for all its meager worth.

Blaine was in court from time to time defending himself and his possession of the farm from suits filed by the King grandparents and by his debtors. Once, before bringing Blaine and the children into court, Mrs. King had sent for her granddaughter Hannah. She received the girl "so piteously clothed that [she] was almost naked [and] so covered with vermin, which had eaten into [her] skin, so that the child would not have lived long." Another granddaughter, Elizabeth, aged about three and a half, was also

Students who broke the rules were whipped, just like their elders, as the whipping post waiting outside this Salem schoolhouse shows. From *Old Time Schools and School Books* (New York: Macmillan Co., 1904) by Clifton Johnson.

taken off the farm for inspection and was also "almost naked, with but a small part of a shift on her, and in like condition as her sister in regard to vermin," suffering "very much for food and raiment."

The Graveses said the children had not been provided for in the nine months they'd been there and that "had it not been for their friends through pity taking some of them [the children] from him [Blaine] and relieving them, they might have perished."

The grandparents won custody in 1677, then went after the farm. The county would have given it to them, but Blaine appealed to the high court, where he noted that he paid ten pounds a year in rent for it and, contrary to accusations, would not "dispose of it for rum as the plaintiff from his dirty mouth with other filth cast at me."

SERVANTS AS "BEASTS OF SLAUGHTER"

Children who were servants lived apart from their parents. The lucky ones became de facto members of the families they worked for, and they lived more or less decently; those less lucky had to cope with, at best, benign neglect. The truly unlucky, though, bore heartbreaking mistreatments and endured enough cruelty to shake anyone's faith in human nature.

Martha Stacy was brought by her parents to a Marblehead commissioner (hearer of small cases) in horrible condition—feeble, black and blue and "very much besotted as if she had lost her understanding and speech." They had put her into the service of Joseph Crocker of Newbury, and word of her bad usage had trickled back. Doctors feared for her life. Her parents petitioned for court action but lacked the money to bring a suit. Depositions were taken, however, and neighbors said they'd heard that the girl was beaten and "called vile names." Mrs. Crocker offered the stock response of an abused servant's superior, saying Martha got drunk and fell. The justices urged the Crockers to return the girl to her parents, but the Crockers resisted, saying her parents were poor and kept by the town and "cared not what became of her."

William Sanders, a fatherless servant boy, was repeatedly whipped—once over a hundred stripes in a day—and beaten on the head and kicked. In a special visit from a selectman and a grand juryman, he was found "very black from his shoulders to his hips." One woman looked into it and spoke to his mistress, Elizabeth Jones, who said, "The more people talked of it the worse it would be for the child." Brought in for "shamefully beating" the boy, the couple was ordered to find him another place.

The trend in Salem in 1682 was stringing servants up and *then* beating them. On one hand, the court didn't blame Philip Fowler for beating Richard Parker that way in principle, noting that anyone was justified in giving "meet correction" to a servant and agreeing that the boy deserved it. But the court did disapprove of Fowler's "hanging him up by the heels as butchers do for beasts of slaughter." Fowler was cautioned against "such kind of punishment." Tobiah Taylor was similarly abused by his master, Samuel Bishop, who punished him "by hanging him up in a strange manner [and] cruelly whipping him." Tobiah's wrists were "very much waled and swollen by the cord" and from "hanging by the hands with his legs tied straddling so he could not stir." Three men visited Bishop, who admitted to it, and saw the boy's "many long red marks sixteen hours after the whipping." Bishop's wife said the boy had been coming home drunk, smoking in bed and lying. She also wanted the court to know the Bishops tolerated no offense. For example, when her maidservant, Phoebe Downey, was being "uncivil," her husband "bade her get a rod and whip her as she saw fit," she informed the court.

In desperation, Thomas Bettis knocked on his neighbor Ben Kimball's door one rainy evening. Asked about his business, he "answered hardly at all," Kimball said. Kimball sent him away but found him the next morning in his barn in clothes "too thin for the season" and "quaking with cold." Thomas wound up as a runaway in the custody of the Ipswich court, where his story came out.

Thomas said he could not please his master, John Simmons, who had beaten him for small and frivolous reasons for years. He spoke of his broken head, blood on the floor, dizziness and being beaten while tied to furniture. Once, he said, he couldn't lift his arm yet was ordered back to work nonetheless.

"I have been so abused that I am afraid to live with him anymore or any longer and, if your honors please to order me to live with another master I am willing, but not to live with him," Thomas pleaded. However, another Simmons servant said Thomas was "very rude in the family whenever his master was away," and a neighbor called him "a very naughty boy." On the other side of it, someone else said he had seen Thomas beaten to the point of fainting and bleeding and had seen Simmons whip him "with three cords tied to a stick so that he brought blood, while he asked the boy if he loved him. The boy said yes and he beat him again."

Simmons was advised to "moderation in the usage of his servant" and told to dispose of him if he could find a suitable swap. Meanwhile, Thomas was ordered to return home with his master and recompense him for running away (pay him the value of his lost labor).

A year later, Thomas ran again and stole on his way out. Categorized as "incorrigible," he was sentenced to be whipped and pay treble damages to his victims, and Master Simmons was discharged of his obligation to teach the boy the weaving trade. But Thomas's luck had turned. A new master was found—William Cogswell, who remitted the whipping with forty shillings. Thomas agreed to go home with Cogswell and serve an extra year, plus six months for the value of denying Simmons his labor a second time.

MEAN STREETS

Young John Mascall was found lying in a Salem lane bleeding. The man who found him saw Charles Hill leaving the scene. Asked why he'd hit him, Hill asked why he should be afraid of a boy and said he'd hit him again. It cost Hill a whipping, five pounds to the boy, five pounds to the boy's master for lost time and the doctor's fee.

A brutal mugging in Lynn in 1688 sent Ralph King Jr. to his death a week after it happened. Two other Lynn residents, John Newhall and Thomas Witt, for no stated reason, "did strike, kick, stamp, and crush" King, giving him "many grievous [sic] and mortal wounds and bruises of which...he did greviously languish." King's death and their malice got the pair charged with murder, but they were convicted only of manslaughter (Newhall) and accessory to manslaughter (Witt). Newhall paid over thirty-six pounds; Witts paid eighteen.

The use of weapons rarely appears in the record, which reveals only a couple of shootings, both ruled accidental, and only a couple of drawn blades. John Clark put a knife to Jestin John's ribs and said if it was sharp enough he'd thrust it into his body; he was whipped for attempting murder on the Lord's Day. William Russell, a servant of Philip English, earned a whipping when, in the middle of cleaning fish, he ran swearing "without provocation" at his captain with a knife. The captain was not injured, but another man was cut as Clark was restrained.

Biters, who can attack without warning, are in their way even more chilling than someone holding a knife. The devious Andrew Wiggins approached Captain Walter Barefoot and, "under pretence of love, bit him in the face." Wiggins avoided a forty-shilling fine by publicly acknowledging his freakish deed.

A Hampton constable, Will Fuller, was bitten by Eunice and William Cole when he went to serve them an execution and seize some of their goods. Eunice cried, "Murder! Murder!" as Fuller approached and said he was "as bad as any of them." They bit his hands trying to get their goods back.

Mary Somes, John Jackson Sr.'s maid, had a better reason for baring her teeth: she was fending him off. She said she was afraid to enter her own chamber and that Jackson had "offered her uncleanness four times, when her dame was abroad." Finally, "the old man tried to kiss her and she bit his nose." He was fined for attempted assault and filthy speeches. She was presumably freed from his lecherous designs forever.

Family Fights

Among Puritan wife-beaters, who appeared in court fairly regularly, Richard Praye was one of the worst. One visitor to his house at the Lynn ironworks, Jabis Hackett, often heard him call his wife Mary "jade" (a worn out, useless horse) and "roundhead" (slang for a Puritan, which implies the Prayes were not), curse her and wish a plague and a pox on her. Hackett said Praye told him he'd beat her "twenty times a day before she should be his master." One day, while she was putting her waistcoat on, Praye lifted her sleeve to show "two great places black and blue." Others saw Praye kick her and hit her arm so hard with a porridge dish "she feared it was broken." When someone told Praye the court would not allow him to abuse his wife like that, he said he did not care for the court, and if the court hanged him for it he would still do it. Told that the court would "make him care, for they had tamed as stout hearts as his," he answered that if he ever had trouble about abusing his wife, "he would cripple her and make her sit on a stool, and there he would keep her." Praye was fined ten shillings for swearing, another ten for cursing, twenty for beating his wife and forty for contempt of court—in total, enough to buy a cow. Mary was feisty, herself. She was admonished and fined two shillings for throwing stones at her mother-in-law and telling her to "get home you old hog," and for throwing a bone at her husband for stealing a letter.

Another wife was the abuser, not the abused, as her husband, Hugh Brown, could attest to. His wife got a severe whipping for "breaking his head and threatening to kill him, so that he is ever weary of his life, throwing stones at him, causing his face to bleed, calling him a beast, and wishing him hanged and that he might never come home." She also annoyed the neighbors, who often had to watch the Browns scuffle.

Being stubborn and rebellious was a deadly serious offense, so father-son conflicts rarely resulted in physical attacks on parents, and no one from Essex was ever executed for them. But John Porter Jr. came as close as can be. Closer than James White, who in 1657, after being struck by his father, got whipped for holding an andiron up and, when asked what he was going to do with it, saying his father "should know by and by." And closer than Richard Martyn, who got ten stripes at the Hampton meetinghouse in 1669 for throwing his father down, stripping him and holding an axe to him.

Young Porter was a contradiction: a Puritan *and* a spoiled brat. He plagued his family for years, eventually driving his father, the richest man in Salem, to try and have him executed. Porter Jr. first appears in the record in 1661, full of phony contrition in a letter from the Ipswich jail, where he was being held for profane, unnatural and abusive carriages to his parents and for abusing their authority. Incarceration inspired him to lament the "strange distance" between them, he wrote. He also lamented the shame, sorrow and penury he was suffering. He expressed "real humility and unfeigned submission, [and was] ready to forgive and forget," and added, "I detest and abhor all my miscarriages." Signed "dutiful son," such bald pretense did not go unnoticed by the high court later, which in a different case pointed out that, despite those alleged sentiments, Porter "did persist in his former course." The letter was a remarkable contrast to the deposition Morgan Jones had given earlier, saying he'd heard Porter call his father "Robin Hood and hypocrite" and his mother a hypocrite with a tongue that "goes like a perriemonger." (A *peri* is a supernatural being descended from fallen angels; a *monger* sells things, sometimes of a discreditable nature.)

That time, young Porter got off with a fine. But then he went into the Boston jail, sent there to face the high court on the capital charge of being stubborn and rebellious, of forfeiting his bond for breach of the peace and, again, for rebellious and abusive carriages to his parents. He had been terrifying his family for months with threats, including one on his father's life, and had tried to stab his brother. The high court described him as a bachelor (never a good thing) of about thirty engaged in "riotous living" who was "instigated by the devil" with a "corrupt heart destitute of the fear of God."

"Riotous living" stemmed from Porter's squandering of some £400 of his father's money, a Puritan fortune, living it up in Barbados and England. The prodigal son, who had likely been paid to just go away, had been jailed for debt in England and released with the help of his father's friends there. Back home, he was characterized as a profane drunkard and proved it by calling his father "thief, liar, simple ape, and shittabed." He threatened to burn down the house, take down the barn and kill the cattle and horses, and in fact did chop down a fence and ignite a pile of wood near the house. He called his grandmother "rambeggur [buggerer of rams], gammar [grandmother] shithouse, gammer pisshouse, gammar two shoes, and the rankest sow in town." He also reviled and beat his father's servants.

At trial, Porter "impudently denied some things," excused some "by vain pretences" and owned up to others but gave no sign of repentance. He would have been executed as his father wished but was saved by his mother's pleading. He stood on the gallows ladder with a rope around his neck for an hour, was severely whipped and returned to jail "to be kept closely to work." He was not to be released without special order of the high court or the Great and General Court (the legislature) and was to pay a £200 fine. But he escaped to Warwick, Rhode Island, where he complained of injustice and received protection pending a rehearing of his case.

(Porter would have found little sympathy back in Massachusetts, even a century later. Massachusetts chief justice Thomas Hutchinson's 1768 charge to the grand jury sadly recalled earlier days, when "a refractory, disobedient child, if he continued obstinate and incorrigible after admonition and reproof, was punished by whipping very severely; and, if that punishment did not reclaim or work some reformation, he was put to death. I can't but regret that we have departed so far from the Spirit of our Fathers, under the old charter, as that a refractory, disobedient child has become so common among us as scarce to be noticed.")[11]

Porter, mean as a snake, at least never killed anyone we know of. But the deadly characters to come did. They aren't Essex's only killers but are among its most wicked because some of their victims, being defenseless, could not have been less deserving of their fate.

Killing, Confession and the Unconscionable

S ome things are rare yet inevitable, like a bit of pleasant weather in the depths of the New England winter. Other things, less pleasant but also inevitable, come from the depths of the New England ocean—corpses. In either case, it's not a question of *if* the next one will appear, only when.

Europeans started washing up on Essex shores from the outset. Sometimes they were strangers, stripped of their boots and left to the crabs, which was regarded as theft, even though they were dead, and frowned upon. They were duly recorded as drowning victims or, when injured, as victims of foul play. The circumstances of their death were nearly always mysterious.

But it was a killing on land for which the county's first murderer, John Williams, was prosecuted.

Williams was a ship's carpenter from England who had

> *lately come into the country and, put in prison for theft, brake [sic] out with one John Hoddy, whom, near the great pond, in the way to Ipswich, he murdered, and took away his clothes and what else he had, and went in them to Ipswich, where he had been sent to prison, and was there again apprehended; and though his clothes were all bloody, yet he would confess nothing, till about a week after the body of Hoddy was found.*[12]

The "great pond" is now called Wenham Lake. Williams was hanged in Boston on September 28, 1637.

Hugh and Hannah Stone had several children and were expecting another when they went out walking one April evening in Andover. They may have set out pleasantly enough, but they got into a quarrel about selling a piece of land, and Hugh slit his wife's throat.

"The wretched man was too soon surprised by his neighbors to be capable of denying the fact, and so he pleaded guilty upon his trial," wrote Cotton Mather in his *Magnalia*.[13]

Stone was hanged on January 2, 1690, and Hannah Hutchinson, wife of Samuel Hutchinson, also of Andover, was tried for (though acquitted of) "feloniously and maliciously" exciting and abetting Hugh the day before the killing.

In the *Magnalia* (quoted here to the end of Hugh's story), Mather reports the conversation between Hugh, just back from his sentencing in Boston and en route to his hanging in Andover, and a minister walking him to his death. Mather's report is more likely an idealized representation of what a typical exchange between a minister and a condemned murderer should be, given how it mainly affirms that mankind is born hopelessly depraved and can be saved only through the belief that the price of its sin was prepaid by the death of Christ.

"Are you sensible that you were born a sinner?" asked the minister. "That the guilt of the first sin committed by Adam is justly charged upon you? And that you have hereupon a wicked nature in you, full of enmity against all that is holy, and just and good? For which you deserved to be destroyed as soon as you first came into this world?"

Hugh answered yes on all counts.

"Are you further sensible that you have lived a very ungodly life? That you are guilty of thousands of actual sins, every one which deserves the wrath and curse of God? Both in this life and that which is to come?"

Again Hugh answered yes.

"But are you sensible that you have broken all the laws of God? You know the commandments. Are you sensible that you have broken every one of them?"

"I cannot answer yes to that. My answer may be liable to some exceptions," Hugh replied.

Asked which commandment he dared categorize as unbroken, Hugh responded, "That commandment, 'thou shalt not make to thy self any graven image.' How have I broken it?"

"Thus: you have had undue images of God in your mind a thousand times."

"Indeed, Sir, I confess it. I see my sinfulness greater than I thought it was."
"You better see it. God help you to see it! There is a boundless ocean of it."
Mather concluded, "After this, he was, by the prayers of a minister then present, recommended to the divine mercy. Which being done the poor man poured out a few broken ejaculations, in the midst of which he was turned over into that eternity which we must leave him in."

And so Hugh Stone met his end.

More tragic are the slain newborns, who never had a chance.

The infanticide that went on colony-wide is one of the record's more surprising revelations and shows how dangerous the seventeenth century was for an illegitimate infant. The stigma of being a loose woman was so complete a condemnation, so certain a path to ruin, it could override what is alleged to be the strongest instinct of all—motherly love and protection. Tiny bodies were secreted away in attics, in the ground and in ponds, where they were found at the bottom with stones tied around their necks.

One Essex woman who risked everything and made that most horrid choice was Elizabeth Emerson, the unmarried daughter of Michael Emerson.

Hester Prynne, from Nathaniel Hawthorne's *The Scarlet Letter*, and her illegitimate daughter, Pearl. Wearing an "A" for adultery was more than some unwed mothers could bear. Artist unknown. From *Romance and Reality of the Puritan Coast* (Boston: University Press, 1897) by Edmund H. Garrett.

Elizabeth gave birth to two children in her father's Haverhill house in the spring of 1691 during the night between Thursday, May 7, and Friday, May 8. She killed them, sewed them into a small cloth bag and hid them in the house until the Sabbath, May 10, when she buried them in the yard. She was found out and paid with her life on September 26.

Esther Rogers of Newbury confessed to killing her second illegitimate child in 1700, after the first had been secreted away, "she not knowing whether it was dead or alive." Esther was hanged and gibbeted—left to twist in the wind as food for thought, and the birds—at Pingrey's Plain in Ipswich. Because she "cast her soul upon Christ"[14] while passing a hill en route to her execution, it was named Comfort Hill. (Pirates were sometimes gibbeted on a small island at the entrance to Boston Harbor, left as lessons to others.)

Another mother killed her child out of apparent madness, not shame, which tempers her coldbloodedness a bit. Puritans didn't have phrases like "mentally disturbed," so Dorothy Talby was instead considered "melancholy"[15] and "distracted," as Winthrop notes in his journal (quoted from here to this chapter's end). Dorothy is now thought to have suffered from postpartum depression, spurred by the birth of her last daughter, one of four children. Things had not augured well when Dorothy named her doomed daughter Difficulty. At wit's end, she took the three-year-old into the woods and snapped her neck. She confessed freely and showed no remorse.

The Talbys had lived in Salem as well-regarded church members for a few years, but Dorothy developed a "difference" with her husband, John, through melancholy and "spiritual delusions." She started fighting with her husband and neighbors and was admonished for it by her church. But her behavior worsened, and in 1636 she was chained to a post for attempted murder or, as the record puts it, for "frequent laying hands on her husband to the danger of his life," and for condemning the authority of the court to punish her.

Then she started obeying "divine revelations" that told her to starve her family and herself. Things worsened when she was excommunicated. Continued assaults on her husband got her whipped, and for a while she seemed to improve. But the revelations returned, and finally "she was so possessed by Satan that he persuaded her [by his delusions, which she listened to as revelations from God,] to break the neck of her own child." She did it, she said, to free the girl "from future misery."

Dorothy said nothing at her arraignment, which led Winthrop to threaten her with the standard procedure for those who refused to plead—death by pressing (see "Meanies, Creeps and Ne'er-do-wells"). Hearing that, she

Hangings weren't frequent enough to warrant a gallows in every town, so the condemned were simply "turned off" a ladder. Artist unknown. *Courtesy Danvers Archival Center.*

confessed and asked to be beheaded, seeing that as less painful and shameful than hanging. She was refused.

Upon hearing her sentence, she neither expressed remorse nor stood and had to be dragged to the gallows, where she again refused to stand. She was somehow forced up the ladder, where the hangman covered her face with a cloth, which she took off and used to protect her neck from the rope instead. When she was "turned off" she swung a time or two, then grasped for the ladder. To no avail. She died slowly, by strangulation, on December 6, 1638, the first woman executed in Massachusetts.

Dorothy's husband was eventually excommunicated, too, for "unnaturalness to his wife" and "much pride."

Murder is one way to prove how cheaply life can be held. Another is to treat it as a commodity, which treatment was something all the Christian charity and Puritan pontification in the world didn't affect in the slightest, in Essex or anywhere else in the colony.

Brutal Business
in Flesh and Blood

Slavery in what was to become the state of Massachusetts predated the Puritans, who simply legalized it and carried on. It was, after all, a surefire moneymaker *and* biblically justified. It ranks high on today's list of wickedness, and in a remote way, its legacy lives on in Essex. There's a lot of old money in the county, and the older it is the more likely it is that it once may have been connected to the windfalls of human bondage—through no fault of later generations, who certainly had no hand in the business practices of their ancestors.

Big money came to Essex on the backs of slaves by virtue of its connection to the burgeoning slave economies of the West Indies. What made the Golden Triangle golden was black slaves, who could take the heat and hard labor of working sugarcane in the islands. Slaves were fed a lot of cod, quite a bit of it taken by Essex fishermen. Molasses made from the cane fed New England distilleries, and New England rum financed more slaves, who went to the plantations to make more molasses. Everyone who mattered won, and by 1763 rum distilleries were operating throughout Essex. Rum profits helped finance the county's eighteenth-century China clippers, which carried much valuable cargo, including spice (notably pepper in Salem, first brought from Indonesia in 1654). Clipper ship profits financed the industrialization of nineteenth-century New England. And the profits from industrialization financed…and on and on.

To be fair, Essex knew a few things about the other side of slavery, too. Many a mariner from Salem, as likely to be of one race as another, was captured, enslaved and held for ransom by Barbary Coast pirates. And "during the various colonial wars, many Englishmen were taken by the Indians as slaves and sold to the French in Canada."[16]

Indians had always enslaved other Indians defeated in war, so it was business as usual when the Puritans followed suit, starting with Indians taken in the Connecticut land grab known as the Pequot Wars, the conflict that was the real beginning of the end for the American Indian in New England. The Pequot Wars marked the moment when Europeans first got serious about terminating resistance with superior force. Essex men, as militia members, fought throughout the wars, including the defining "battle" of 1637, a one-sided engagement near where Mystic now stands. On May 26, 1637, a group of Pequots, mostly old men, women and children left behind by a traveling war party, were surrounded and driven into their enclosure, which was then set on fire. Carrying what stone age weapons they had, they ran out into muskets and pistols, fired by men in breastplates and helmets. Estimates of their dead that day range from three hundred to seven hundred. The captured warriors and boys—defeated, dangerous and vengeful—were sent to the West Indies to be swapped for more valuable Africans, who had been made docile and were better field workers. Indians "always sank under hard labor," and "in constitution of body and mind" were considered "far below the negro race."[17] They were used as laborers but just as often were servants, craftsmen, hunters, fishermen and guides.[18]

Captured women and children were usually used locally. When Salem minister Hugh Peter got news of the arrival of the prisoners who survived the Connecticut massacre, he wrote Governor Winthrop, who was in charge of doling them out, saying, "We have heard of a dividence [division] of women and children in the bay and would be glad of a share viz: a young woman or girl and a boy if you think good."[19]

A year after the massacre, in the summer of 1638, seventeen Pequots, including two females, boarded the 120-ton *Desire* (built in either Salem or Marblehead, depending on the source) in manacles, part of the cargo for its maiden voyage, as were dried cod and strong liquor. They were bound for sale in Bermuda but wound up in Providence Isle, now New Providence, the island home of Nassau, capital of the Bahamas. The vagaries of wind, information, supplies, politics and other factors often sent vessels off their planned courses. Captain William Pierce's return cargo was cotton, tobacco, salt and "many Negroes" from Tortuga, where he had met two men-of-war who had taken the Africans as a prize from the Spanish. Pierce "secured"

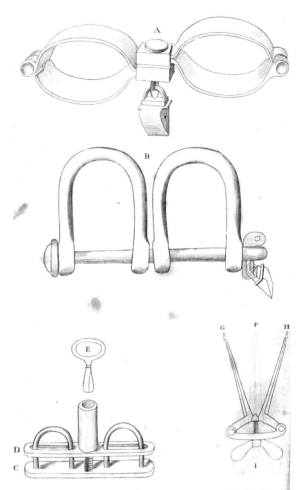

Slave handcuffs, leg shackles, thumbscrews and, at lower right, a speculum oris, which opened the mouths of slaves who wouldn't eat. Forced feeding prevented costly suicides. From *The History of the Rise, Progress, and Accomplishment of the Abolition of the African Slave Trade* (1808) by Thomas Clarkson. *Courtesy American Antiquarian Society*.

the Africans and took them home.[20] The *Desire* had become the colony's first slave ship and the Africans on it the colony's first black slaves.

Puritans eventually outlawed slavery unless, as was written in their code, the Body of Liberties, "it be lawful captives taken in just warres [wars], and such strangers as willingly sell themselves or are sold to us...this exempts none from servitude." That's a jumbo-sized loophole, and it made Massachusetts the first North American colony to formally endorse human trafficking. The law simply "made legal what was already there."[21]

In 1645, Governor Winthrop got another letter from someone who wanted slaves, his brother-in-law, Emmanuel Downing. Downing lobbied for a new Indian war, not against the already ruined and cowed Pequots but, odiously, against the Narragansetts, who had been the Puritans' allies against the Pequots. God's Puritan soldiers could end the "worship of the devil" taking place at powwows, Downing suggested, and at the same time "easily have men, women, and children enough to exchange for Moores," as Africans were called.

"I do not see how we can thrive until we get into a stock of slaves sufficient to do all our business," Downing stated forthrightly, pointing out that "we shall maintain twenty Moores cheaper than one English servant."[22]

Winthrop, in this instance, declined.

And so the Essex record filled up with references to owned persons, but scribes and other members of the elite—except Downing—did not call them slaves. They recorded "servant," "negro" and sometimes "negar" or "neger" instead. A writ in a 1670 case in Salem between William Hollingworth and Michael Powell Jr. refers to "a little Negro boy known by the name of Cesar now in the hands of Mr. William Hollingworth, [being] the proper goods of said Powell." Historian Sidney Perley was less delicate and further implied that Caribs were being taken, too. "There were a considerable number of slaves here, Negroes and West Indians," he wrote.[23]

Governor Simon Bradstreet, variously a resident of Ipswich, Salem and Boston, wrote in 1680 that "one small vessel about two years since, after twenty months' voyage to Madagascar, brought hither betwixt forty and fifty Negroes...most women and children sold here for 15 and 20 [pounds] apiece."[24] That put the value of a slave at the rough equivalent of three or four cows, or a dozen swine or even a modest house, lot and barn. Sometimes slaves were sold by the inch—the taller the pricier.

Prices for Indians in Essex included twenty pounds for "one Indian" and five pounds for "one boy and one girl" in Newbury in 1683. Twenty pounds were paid for a boy and fifteen for a "maid" in Salem in 1684. Another Indian sold for four pounds in Ipswich in 1693.[25] There were some 2,000 slaves in Massachusetts by 1720, including "a few Indians."[26] The Essex County slave tally was 459 in 1754.[27] Ipswich alone had 62 slaves over the age of sixteen in 1755, both Indian and African.[28]

Until the Massachusetts constitution was approved in 1780, buying and selling people was as legal as—and bore striking similarities to—buying and selling fruit, which sells best when not too damaged. The constitution's "free and equal" clause put an end to legalized slavery, "one of the greatest abominations ever chargeable upon the home of the Puritans,"[29] but slave sales in the state continued clandestinely for many years.

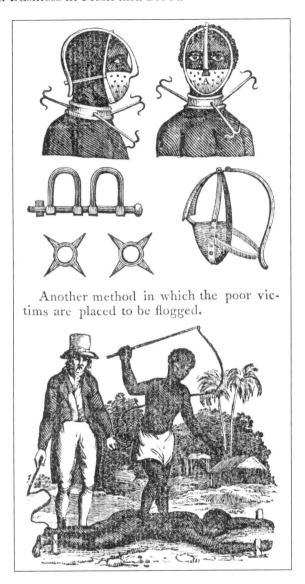

Another method in which the poor victims are placed to be flogged.

The branks silenced
"scolds" and prevented
slaves from unauthorized
eating. From *Injured
Humanity: Being a
Representation of What the
Unhappy Children of Africa
Endure from Those Who
Call Themselves Christians*
(between 1805 and 1808),
an antislavery tract by
Samuel Wood of New
York City. *Courtesy American
Antiquarian Society.*

HEY, THAT'S MY INDIAN!

Slaves legally obtained as spoils of war were one thing, but the law drew the line at *independent* enslavement. "Man stealing," as it was called, was another capital offence. But some freelancers played it fast and loose and got away with it.

Essex residents heard about William Waldron and Henry Lauton in 1677, partners who "did unlawfully surprise and steal away seventeen Indian men,

73

women, and children" at the eastward. The pair put the Indians on the ketch *Endeavour*, sailed to Ffyall (a British Isles port) and sold them. Each entrepreneur successfully pleaded not guilty to man stealing, and the case ended with Lauton guilty of "receiving" the Indians on board and taking them away. Hypocrisy won the day, and his twenty-pound fine was abated to ten. A whiff of palm grease was part of John Hubbard's part in the business. Because part of the "produce" was sold to him, he was charged with "the recovery of said Indians or [what] otherwise upon hearing might appear just." Which meant either bring the Indians home, which was impractical, or make a (cash) settlement with the court, which was more likely.

Some real concern for Indians had been demonstrated a decade earlier, when the Salisbury court told Richard Oliver to "look carefully" that a boy "may not want what is convenient and necessary according to English manner." Oliver had taken an Indian boy without his father's consent. The boy's signature on an indenture was offered as legitimization, but the document was held invalid when its witness proved to be another, older Indian who'd pretended (probably for a fee) to be the boy's uncle. Oliver was ordered to either return the boy or get a certificate of the father's consent, signed by English inhabitants of Nantucket, the boy's home.

Ownership of another Indian boy was warmly contested in 1684.

Captain Daniel Epps of Ipswich, then about sixty, told how a boy came to be his and how he was later taken by another Ipswich resident. Epps's story started about fourteen years earlier, when a group of destitute Indians came to his house. Some had lived on his land before. In the group was an old squaw, Prasqua, from near the lake at the uppermost part of the Merrimack River; her son Robin; and a younger squaw with two sons, one two or three years old and another two or three months old. Prasqua was "past work," and the young woman was "very lame." Because these Indians spoke little English, others explained that "Moquages" had "terribly massacred" the squaws' husbands and another of Prasqua's sons.

The young squaw grew increasingly lame and soon died. She had been "very thankful" to Epps and had said she wanted him to care for her older son, Daniel, who had been given Epps's first name. "And she further said [I] give you my younger son, which she entreated me to accept," Epps said. That boy was called Lionel, which was Epps's son's name.

Epps continued to care for the Indian family for a few years, and as Prasqua's health deteriorated, "she always said 'your boy Lionel' and did constantly own and acknowledge him so to be," he testified.

But Robin, the boys' uncle, complicated things. "Being idle," Epps explained, Robin "ran himself into debt with Henry Bennett, also of Ipswich, and was like to come into trouble [and so] took away my boy when I was [away] from home and put him to said Bennett by writing" to pay his debt. "Put him" meant signing him into servitude.

Bennett produced a signed indenture, dated May 15, 1679, that bound the boy to him for eleven years. It bore the marks of Prasqua, Robin and himself. And Bennett's claim to the boy was supported by others, who confirmed that Prasqua had given her grandson to him to pay Robin's debt and had overridden her now-dead daughter by saying the boy belonged to Bennett.

Epps said the indenture was no more valid than it would be for him to take away and sell one of Bennett's own sons, and his allies rallied. John Ring and Thomas Smith said Bennett only "pretended" he had the boy by indenture. Rebecca Berry, who had lived in the Epps household for several years, confirmed that Prasqua had often said the boy was Epps's. And John Dent, a former apprentice to Epps, confirmed that Epps had given the Indians food and clothing and that Epps's servants had cut firewood for them. In the summer, their wigwam was near the Epps house "and in the winter further off amongst thick pines…where it was much sheltered from all cold winds," Dent said, adding that Epps always helped them set the wigwams up.

"If anyone stealing a boy from another and by writing putting him off to pay their son's debt or debts be legal or warrantable, I think I understand little of law or reason," Epps concluded.

The county court upheld Bennett's document. On appeal, however, the Court of Assistants awarded Epps "the Indian boy in controversy," and ordered the boy or twenty pounds to be delivered within ten days.

Indentured Servitude

Indentured servitude—contract labor for a finite number of years—wasn't quite as bad as slavery. But it, too, could be forced on people who certainly preferred to be otherwise occupied.

When servitude was voluntary, it was considered a fair swap: time served in labor for a trade taught or for eventual freedom, both with room and board included. Boys as young as seven were commonly bound as apprentices to tradesmen for seven, even ten years. Adults bound as laborers worked to pay for their passage to, and eventual liberty in, the New World, usually after three to seven years. But servants were legally subject to physical punishment, and there was little restraint on misuse and cruelty. The years could be hellish and deadly; disease and suicide took many before their time was up. And when it *was* up, some masters would unscrupulously try to extend it.

Like slaves, indentured servants were personal property to be used, sold and inherited. They needed their owner's permission to marry and, in Essex and elsewhere, often had to agree to receive instruction in the Puritan way of life.

Involuntary servitude was just slavery by another name and often began the same way, with the strong preying on the weak. Two Irishmen told their sad story in 1661, having reached their breaking point and, effectively, going on strike, which got them arrested.

William Downing and Philip Welch, ages unknown, were "stolen in Ireland, by some of the English soldiers, in the night out of their beds and brought to Mr. [George] Dell's ship…against their consents." On board were "others of their countrymen, weeping and crying, because they were stolen from their friends," they told the court.

The stolen Irish were brought across the ocean, and Downing and Welch were sold to Mr. Symonds of Salem. After seven years, a common period of servitude, they went to Mrs. Symonds and said, "We will work with you, or for you, no longer."

"Is it so?" Mrs. Symonds said. "What will you, play?"

"We have served you seven years, we think that is long enough," they replied.

"We must not be our own judges," put in Mr. Symonds condescendingly, telling the pair they had to work "until you run away."

Running would make them fugitives, of course, and subject to whippings. They said they would run anyway but also offered an alternative.

"If you will free us, we will plant your corn and mend your fences if you will pay us as other men, but we will not work with you upon the same terms or conditions as before."

Symonds suggested they all pray over it.

"You may go to prayer, we will speak more in the morning," Downing replied.

The morning brought precious little conversation. The pair was greeted by a constable and three deputies and arrested. When they asked to see by what authority they were being kept, Symonds "produced a writing, which, he said, was all he had to show for them." The writing, which they probably couldn't read anyway, could have set any number of conditions.

Brutal Business in Flesh and Blood

Roger Conant was Salem's first Puritan settler. The area was then called Naumkeag, the tribal name of its original inhabitants. By the sculptor Henry H. Kitson, 1911. *Author photo.*

The resolution of the Irishmen's case is unknown, but they may have had some reason for hope, however remote. John Eggon, three years later, successfully complained to the same court about having been sold to several masters, with the result of several years added to his time, "more than of right ought to be." The court voided all sales of Eggon but his first.

FROM PRISONER TO SERVANT AND SERVANT TO VICTIM

Involuntary servitude was also the fate of many culprits who were unable to pay their fines.

Hugh Hancock was censured in 1666 for swearing, whipped and jailed for unruly carriage and convicted of threatening to kill his master and offering "gross abuses" to his dame. Unable to pay ten pounds to the county and twelve to his master for lost time, he was committed to the Ipswich prison until his sale could cover those costs.

In 1674, "Tom Indian Robins assaulted a woman and her daughter and was fined five pounds." He was told he would be sold if it were not paid within a week. A year later, Major William Hathorne noted the county's disposal of the money received "from the sale of Thomas Robins, the Indian."

Essex convicts John Kelly and John Kendall were sold in the frigid winter of 1685–86, partially for mercy's sake. Kelly, in jail for stealing linens, was allowed to sell himself because the victims had gotten the linens back and the winter was "proving violent cold and [there were] no chimneys in prison." To get the country "well rid of a grand thief," he was sent as a servant to Barbados "for three pounds ten shillings for four years service." A month later, Kendall, in for stealing three horses, also faced freezing to death. "Not having any estate," he was sold off to Barbados, too.

The abuses of servants are beyond counting, mainly because they rarely made it into the justice system. Those who faced their masters and dames in court were the tip of the iceberg and usually learned that the system believed masters before it believed them and treated masters leniently. In general, the court advised moderation in discipline but also recognized the need to apply "meet correction."

In 1645, Daniel Rumble's hammer came down on his servant Henry Hall's head. It was a fatal blow, in part because it was "so long before it was dressed." (Rumble had previously appeared for giving Hall fifty blows, presumably with something other than a hammer.) George Emery supported Rumble's claim that the hammer strike was an accident, testifying that Rumble told him he had been driving a nail into a door or a shutter and somehow Hall's skull accidentally got in the way, which is, theoretically, at least conceivable—bad aim, perhaps. Rumble's sentence seemed lenient, given that it implied the incident was not seen as an accident: he was fined and admonished for cruelty in "correcting" his "late servant."

Thomas and Naomi Maule also had little to fear from Puritan justice. They were charged in 1681 with cruelly beating Joan Sullivan, their "poor Irish servant woman." Joan said her master had many times "unreasonably beat me with an unlawful weapon to strike a Christian, which weapon is by the English called a maunatee, or horse whip, sometimes thirty or forty blows at a time and sometimes before my clothes have been on about me." She said she spit blood for a fortnight, lived in fear for her life and was forced to work on the Sabbath.

Hannah Sibley said she had seen Joan's face bloody and swollen. John Flint, another Maule servant, "heard a great cry in the house and, looking in, saw Naomi Maule beating and thumping [Joan] on the head in a very violent manner and also kicking her." Naomi, he said, told Joan that when her master came home he would give her ten times as much.

Mistress Naomi claimed she had only struck Joan with a light touch on the ear, which made her "run roaring" into the street. Others pointed to Joan's alleged theft, malice and provoking language; one said she was "a most wicked servant for inventing lies."

The Sullivan case was dismissed.

Private "correction" was one thing. Over half a century, nearly two dozen Essex servants were also *publicly* punished for stubbornness, disobedience and running away. In the process, some bizarre moments and wild images came to light.

John Cooke, a servant to William Clark of Salem, was severely whipped and shackled in 1640 for resisting Clark's authority and putting him and his wife in fear of their lives with "most desperate speeches." In court, Cooke pointed to his side and told the judges "you shall see a hole here first" and that he would have more company if he were in hell.

Elizabeth Johnson, a servant to Joseph Young, was severely whipped and fined five pounds in 1642 for "unseemly practices between her and another maid," "stubbornness to her mistress," "answering rudely and unmannerly," "stopping her ears with her hands when the word of God was read," "spurning" a ewe and baby goat "until both died" and "killing a pig and burying it."

Henry Spencer ran from Edmond Mounforth in 1665 after stealing a coat, some clothing, some serge, two Bibles and a rapier. He got to Andover, where he broke into a house and stole a horse and saddle. After his capture, he compounded his troubles by breaking out of Ipswich prison. Spencer was severely whipped and branded on the forehead with a "B." He also paid five pounds to the county, treble damages (thirteen pounds) for the thefts and forty shillings for lost time and went to the Boston prison until Mounforth could dispose of him.

But no servant in Essex ran like Nick Vauden. Between 1666 and 1670, he parted company with Robert Crose three times. The first time he was whipped for running away and breaking out of prison and had to return what he had stolen and pay double its value to his victims. The second time he was whipped severely, had an iron put around his neck and was fined five pounds for his hue and cry and another fifteen for Crose, who was given the right to sell him for ten years "to any English nation." The third time he was returned with an iron around his neck, severely whipped, branded on the forehead with an "R" (presumably for runaway) and ordered to pay an extraordinary forty pounds to Crose, enough for a large farm, or four teams of oxen.

Servants paid a heavy price for running away, whether or not they were justified. Whether their flights were well planned or they acted spontaneously, all they could really expect as fugitive runaways was an outlaw's life or that of a castaway in a wilderness filled with Indians, or maybe a seaman's berth, which could well mean replacing one harsh master with another. The enormity of the gamble met the enormity of the desperation.

Those who gambled and ran despite everything must have found it passing strange that others, those curious Quakers, also risked everything—not to get away from Puritans, but to get so deeply in among them as to contest the contents of their hearts.

The Deadly Wrath of God's Gatekeepers

The noble-sounding quest for religious freedom is what brought the Puritans to Massachusetts, first and foremost. But it was only *their* religious freedom they were after, and they wasted no time in establishing a theocracy violently intolerant of non-Puritan ideas. Religious freedom as we know it today was not at all what they had in mind.

It was their mission and duty to purify the church and bring others to that purity, and in their zeal they stopped at nothing, as the Quakers who dared contest their theology found out.

Puritan ministers, often graduates of England's best universities, founded Harvard in 1636 so they could produce more like themselves. They were more intellectual, hierarchical and authoritarian than the relatively egalitarian Pilgrims to the south. Access to God went through *them*, and they were jealous gatekeepers; nothing threatened and outraged ministers more than the idea that no one needed their guidance to get in and see Him…that they were *unnecessary*. But that was exactly what the Quakers said—that God is directly accessible to everyone, no intermediaries required, only "inner light." If that was true, ministers were irrelevant. Little wonder then that when the first Quakers landed in Boston in 1656 they were arrested, checked for witch's marks and banished under pain of death dare they return.

Most of them went to Rhode Island and stayed there. Four returned to Massachusetts, including Salem, to test the Puritan resolve, knowing full well they were entering hostile territory yet ready to suffer and die for their beliefs. As subverters of the theocracy, Quakers were beyond wicked; they were anathemas. Even worse, some everyday Puritans were starting to open up to the Quaker point of view. It had to be stopped. Briefly, it was, and in the process something significant was revealed about the Puritan interpretation of "Thou shalt not kill." It wasn't an all-or-nothing commandment for them. It didn't apply to war, it didn't apply to sanctioned retribution and it didn't apply to annoying Quakers.

The official reason the Quakers were executed was because they violated their banishments. In essence, they were said to be hanged for trespassing, but that was only half the story. The General Court's declaration upon the occasion of the 1659 hanging of Quakers William Robinson and Marmaduke Stevenson was another attempt to have things both ways, like outlawing slavery with exceptions so broad they made the law practically meaningless. In regards to the men about to die, the court hypocritically said "we desire their lives absent, rather than their deaths present." And the court gave King Charles II, who had recently replaced Puritan superman Oliver Cromwell as the head of England, half the truth, disingenuously explaining that "the Quakers died, not because of their other crimes...but upon their superadded presumptuous and incorrigible contempt of authority; breaking in upon us, notwithstanding their [previous] sentence of banishment."

But the Quaker executions *were* about "their other crimes" and were decidedly unpopular. To be safe, soldiers were brought in for crowd control—a hundred at one of the hangings. But the hangings only brought the genie farther out of the bottle, creating martyrs and increasing popular support. Quakers died with cheerful dignity, turning the moral tables by using their gallows as platforms for faith and courage. En route to their deaths, they encouraged the crowd to find the same intellectual and spiritual freedom they had. The effort to silence them reached all the way to the noose as drummers drowned out their last words to all but those close enough to hear.

From jail, Robinson and Stevenson had written:

> *Oh, thou New England...is thy religion come to no more than whipping, imprisoning, burning in the hand, and cutting off ears, and banishing upon death?...Is thy praying, thy preaching, thy many sacrifices, and vain oblations, come to this? Blush and be ashamed...Oh ye hypocrites! How can you sing, and keep such a noise concerning religion, when your hands are full of blood? Thou boasts in thy wickedness, and thinks thou doest God good service, to hang and put to death the people called Quakers... Oh you heads and rulers...who are become so brutish, and so dark in*

The Deadly Wrath of God's Gatekeepers

your understandings…If you do put us to death, this action of yours will proceed from the Devil, who was a murtherer from the Beginning.[30]

The Quaker George Bishop was on Boston Common for the hangings and poignantly described the pair's last moments, which were spent with another condemned Quaker, Mary Dyer. They went "to the place of execution, hand in hand, all three of them, as to a wedding day, with great cheerfulness of heart; and having taken leave of each other, with the dear embraces of one another, in the love of the Lord...died...full of the joy of the Lord...their countenances not changing."[31] Dyer's sentence was commuted at the last moment, but she was returned and hanged another day.

In 1661, the Court of Assistants executed the Quaker William Leddra, who had visited Salem three years earlier. Leddra told the court he "owed no subjection [to] wicked laws" and "would not own [this] governor to be his judge."[32] He had been imprisoned for a year, chained to a log the whole time and returned to court to make his final speech with the log in tow.

"I know your ministers are deluders and yourselves murderers," Leddra told the colony's most powerful men, "and if I ever turn to such murderers as you are let all this company say I have turned from God...and this I will seal with my blood."[33]

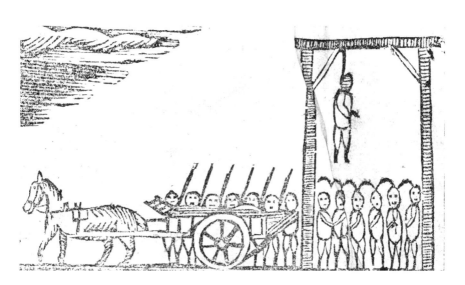

A hanging as depicted by an unknown Boston artist, circa 1737. From *A Dictionary of Colonial American Printers' Ornaments & Illustrations* (American Antiquarian Society, 1975) by Elizabeth Carroll Reilly. *Courtesy American Antiquarian Society.*

Leddra was the last Quaker to hang. In the fall of that year, a directive from the king put an end to Quaker executions. Jailings, whippings and other nonlethal yet savage persecutions continued. A handbill, certainly posted surreptitiously, listed Quaker ears cut off, hands burned with an "H" (for heretic), whippings of hundreds of stripes and beatings that turned bodies into something "like a jelly."

ESSEX QUAKERS

The first arrest of Quakers and Quaker sympathizers in Essex came on Sunday, May 4, 1658, when a "disorderly meeting" at Nicholas Phelps's house in Salem was raided. The arrests were for "absence from public worship and the service of God." Leddra and another Quaker, William Brend, escaped but were soon caught. Members of the Phelps, Southwick, Shadduck, Pope, Trask, Buffum and other families were at the meeting. Some of those arrested exercised passive resistance by not removing their hats in court "til by the officer they were pulled off." Some were fined. Others repented and were released. Still others called the justices "persecutors" and went in the stocks for an hour. Four were whipped. Those who confessed to being Quakers were "convicted of the evil of their ways and practices" and taken to the Boston jail.

From there, on May 16, the group wrote the Salem judges, calling them "Friends" in the Quaker fashion and noting they had done "nothing worthy of stripes or bonds." Their incarceration was ruining their farms and livestock, they wrote, but "we know if the spirit of Christ did dwell and rule in you these things would take impression on your hearts…What we now suffer for is much from false reports and ungrounded jealousy of heresy and sedition." They were "made willing in the power and strength of God freely to offer up our lives in this cause of God," they added.

Those imprisoned, and their families, along with other Quaker sympathizers in Essex, were repeatedly arrested, rearrested, fined, imprisoned and physically punished time after time for "persisting still in their course as Quakers." The persecution ruined many, including the Southwicks of Salem. In 1658, Lawrence and Cassandra Southwick were banished. Left behind were their children, Daniel, twenty-two, and Provided, eighteen. Daniel and Provided continued the family practice of boycotting Puritan services. Provided allegedly fanned the flames with her "contemptuous and presumptuous carriage at

Salem to the great disturbance of the peace." Fined and imprisoned for failure to pay, the court ordered the pair sold in 1659. Provided's unpaid fine was forty shillings, the price of a dining room set. They were brought onto the Salem wharves and "offered for sale as slaves to the sea captains who might carry them to the West Indies and dispose of them at a profit. But no one would buy them; and the brother and sister were released."[34]

The wife of Anthony Needham (too unimportant to be fully named, as wives often were) upped the anti-authoritarian ante in 1660. Fined three pounds and six shillings by Essex judges for fifteen days' absence from public ordinances (church services), she refused to pay. She also refused to have the fine paid *for* her and insisted on having "the punishment inflicted upon her person," using her twelve stripes as an obvious and dramatic statement about Puritan injustice. (Constable Thomas Roots earned a significant two pounds and sixpence for whipping her, presumably for the distastefulness of the task.) Later, the Southwicks and John Bleven, also being punished for nonattendance, followed Needham's lead and insisted on being whipped, too.

Another form of Quaker passive disobedience appeared in Essex in 1663, a banner year for Quaker protest in the county. The new disobedience was also dramatic and also forced the authorities to reveal their true natures. Women appeared in church and on the street as God made them, naked as they day they were born. Their message was that like newborns, they, as Quakers, were innocent, harmless and without shame. Robert Wilson's wife, Deborah, of Salem, was one of them. She was sentenced "for her barbarous and unhuman going naked through the town," and—without irony—stripped to the waist, tied to a cart's tail "and whipped from [Salem tavern keeper] Mr. Gidney's gate to her own house, not exceeding thirty stripes, and her mother Buffum and sister Smith, her abettors, to be tied on either side of her naked to their shifts to the waist, and accompany her." Lidia Wardell, whose husband had been persecuted for Quaker sympathies, was whipped for walking naked into the Newbury meetinghouse.

Eliahim Wardell had the temerity to tell the "worshipful Mr. Bradstreet, as he sat on the bench, in the face of the country, that he was malicious and had 'instanced' the death of four friends"—the hanged Quakers. Wardell was whipped "fifteen stripes at the common whipping place this present afternoon, at the court's coming to the house again." In other words, right after lunch. Samuel Shaddock was ordered fined or whipped the same day, for charging "court and country" with being guilty of shedding "innocent blood," as was Philip Vern, whipped for slander, having said the government had murdered the dear saints and servants of God and that he himself had seen one die. Vern went into the stocks, too, for disowning the country's power to force anyone "to come to the public worship." The year 1663 also saw Quaker land seized for use as a prison site in Salem, and the court appearance of a Salem resident who had invited all his neighbors, including his Puritan minister, to a Quaker meeting.

The governor himself was "guilty in shedding innocent Quaker blood," said Nathaniel Hadlock in 1668. Hadlock boldly added that he'd been at three Quaker meetings and profited more from them than from hearing the minister John Higgeson. For that, he was admonished, fined and severely whipped. Edward Wharton was fined fifty pounds and imprisoned that year for coming into court irreverently and contemptuously, refusing to remove his hat and charging the government with unrighteousness, cruelty and the shedding of innocent blood.

No God, No Devil, No Hell

Feelings about the Quaker executions continued to run high in Essex for many years. Marbleheader Joseph Gatchell drew on them in 1675, during the great Indian uprising called King Philip's War, the tribes' desperate effort, forty years after the Connecticut massacre, to reclaim their homeland. It was the scariest and most violent time in memory. Half of New England's towns, including many on the Essex frontier like Andover and Haverhill, were attacked. All colonists at the eastward were either killed, held captive or scared out. Providence, Rhode Island, was abandoned and burned to the ground. Gruesome stories came out of the woods, stories about "men and women soaked in blood appearing at a neighbor's house only to die, screaming in agony, on the doorstep of a family too terrified to let them in."[35]

Gatchell, a Salem tailor, was a loose cannon. Known to consort with thieves, he was a "waterfront brawler" who "enjoyed shocking his more staid neighbors with occasional blasphemies and overt defiance of magistrates and constables."[36] At a gathering at Goodman Prince's home, he said the current Indian wars were "the judgment of God upon us" for murdering Quakers. He made a run for it when he learned he had been reported for saying that. His search warrant directed the Marblehead and Salem constables "to search any house where you think him to be and if denied to break open any

Inland Essex was Indian country, where frontier women fought alone. By John Boyle, Boston, 1773. From *A Dictionary of Colonial American Printers' Ornaments & Illustrations* (American Antiquarian Society, 1975) by Elizabeth Carroll Reilly. *Courtesy American Antiquarian Society.*

doors, closets, and chests." He was caught and sentenced to a whipping or a fine for "speaking reproachfully and contemptuously."

But Gatchell wasn't nearly done. In 1680, he was fined and imprisoned for "reviling and reproachful speeches against the magistrates and ministry." They "made a game of praying," he had said, and the minister John Higginson "bawled like a bear." He also claimed the Scriptures were the words of men, not God, but were presented as such "to make simple people believe so, to keep them in ignorance." *He* knew better and considered himself a Quaker, he added. His imprisonment was respited when he pleaded his wife's weakness, his child's youth and his inability to provide for them while in jail. If he was kept there, he said, "wife and babe must perish, trade spoiled, custom lost."

Gatchell paid most dearly four years later, when he brought upon himself the more serious charge of "blasphemous and atheistical speeches denying that there is either a God or devil or hell." During a discourse on salvation, someone said that Christ sent his disciples out to preach that whoever repents and believes shall be saved. "If it be so, he was an imperfect savior and a fool," Gatchell replied. That brought him before the Court of Assistants, where "after many refusals" he finally pleaded not guilty. He was taken "to the pillory to have his head and hand put in and have his tongue drawn forth out of his mouth and pierced through with hot iron and then returned to prison." Gatchell stayed there until seven pounds in charges and fees were paid, knowing they could have hanged him.

OTHER CRACKS IN THE DOCTRINAL VENEER

The Puritan guard faced its first religious provocations in Essex in 1642, twelve years after the fleet landed—a blink of history's eye and long before any Quakers showed up. It turns out that behind all the fire and brimstone was a surprising amount of religious discord, even disrespect, ranging from sarcastic to brazen to vehement, and all of it wicked, naturally. It shows that Puritans were *not* homogenous, nor in lockstep with a common belief, nor predictable. There were free thinkers among them, willing to attack the state religion and its ministers, Harvard educated or not. Not for nothing was mutiny a crime in churches as well as on vessels, in forts and anywhere else in the military.

First to be questioned was the first sacrament: baptism. Specifically, infant baptism. Many in Essex neither believed in nor practiced it, and they started getting called into court for failing to baptize their infants in 1642, when Lady Deborah Moody of Lynn, apparently willing to start a trend, appeared on the docket for it (with no recorded outcome). Others so charged—and their numbers grew quickly—were most often admonished, but some were threatened with prison if they didn't conform. These "criminals" were not specifically identified as Anabaptists but were acting in concert with that long-persecuted sect. Anabaptists were not against baptism, they just thought it should wait and be given to those able to comprehend its meaning. Infants, they thought, were simply unable to grasp it. Thomas Cooke chose between a whipping and a fine in 1649 for reproaching infant baptism, saying if he had children, "he would not have them so played the fools withal." Cooke had also claimed that what the minister Mr. Norton taught "was false."

Other Essex church members, and some Essex residents outside the church, were similarly unafraid to challenge the religious establishment and, when necessary, suffer the consequences.

Reverend Cobbett was a minister who, while unpopular with some, held sway over his congregation for several decades. One of his deriders, Henry Walton of Lynn, said in 1643 "he had as leave to hear a dog bark as to hear Mr. Cobbett preach." The wife of Thomas Coates, of Lynn, was brought into court in 1646 for "saying publicly and disturbing those who sat near, when Mr. Cobbett was preaching," that Christ was circumcised on the eighth day and was not baptized. Luke Perkins was whipped in 1681 for saying Cobbett was "more fit to be in a hogsty than in a pulpit, and that he had been a vile man in his former days." Elizabeth Perkins also attacked Cobbett for preaching nothing but "homily," implying his penchant for platitudes and triteness.

Elizabeth Legg attacked her minister, the Reverend Walton, on and off for twenty years. In 1647, she was charged with "reviling" him and was sued by him for it. In 1653, to avoid the stocks, she confessed her sin of again slighting and reproaching him, stating:

> *I, Elizabeth Legg, do acknowledge that I did evil and sinful in speaking slightly and scornful of Mr. Walton, and in particular in saying I could have a boy from the* [Harvard] *college that would preach better than Mr. Walton for half the wages.*

In 1660, Elizabeth said if people followed Walton's preaching they would "all go to hell," and in 1667 she was in court for "making a disturbance in the meeting house." Henry Coombs, another Walton critic, was ordered fined or whipped that year for saying Walton "preached nothing but lies."

There were jokers among the impious, too. John and Stephen Talby were admonished for "unbecoming speeches" in 1644, when they said a dog could not be proven baptized simply by its being in the water. Another dog owner, George Harding, a Marblehead fisherman, had to pay a fine or be whipped in 1649 for stating his intention to join the church so he could have his dog christened.

Dogma was further attacked when Thomas Maule was whipped "ten stripes well laid on" in 1669 for saying Higginson "preached lies" and held "the doctrine of the devil." Nicholas Phelps's wife (one of those arrested in the Salem Quaker raid of 1658) raised hackles in 1661 for saying priests were "deceivers" and Reverend Higginson "sent abroad his wolves and bloodhounds amongst the sheep and lambs."

"Wolves and bloodhounds" meant tithingmen, who were often obnoxious zealots, volunteers who collected money from, spied on and generally kept the congregation—sheep and lambs—in line when it wasn't in church. *In* church, tithingmen were the ones who used sticks to keep snoozers awake. Outside church, they virtually had carte blanche and took the policing of religion as far as they could. They went, as one of them put it, wherever "we suspected rudeness to be." But they, too, met with resistance and were sometimes hit themselves. One woman was asleep in her Beverly home when they visited her for "constantly neglecting public worship." They knocked on her door and woke her daughter, who then woke her. The tithingmen reported that she "let us in, and when we asked about her neglect, said with angry words we had more need to look after rude boys and bid us go out of her house." Another woman, Hannah Mason, was arrested for trying to hit a tithingman with an andiron while drunk. When someone took the andiron away, she tried using a chair "but fell, being unable to stand upon her legs." In 1674, Edward Feaveryear was fined two shillings for abusing the constable who had come to collect the minister's rate (salary share) from him. The constable complained that Feaveryear hit him "violently upon the breast" and was "calling me pimp."

There was discord between parishioners themselves, too, sometimes inside the church, where disruptions, arguing, fighting and stealing were not unknown. In 1674 a group of boys was admonished for "disorder during worship," namely talking, throwing hats and "prating together, sometimes laughing, spitting in one another's faces, pricking one another's legs, jousting boys off their seats, heaving things into the other gallery among the girls who sat there, [and] breaking the glass windows."

Joseph Fowler said in 1649 that there were seven or eight liars in his church and that "if one would lie soundly he was fit for the church."

One place of worship itself went begging for respect. Exeter (then in Essex, now in New Hampshire) was brought to account in 1676 for letting its meetinghouse "lie open and common for cattel to go into." The town was ordered to "make it clean and decent for Christians to meet in" and to make sure that "the doors be hung and kept shut."

When things in the colony weren't going well—a poor harvest, a spreading disease, bad weather or an Indian victory—it was thought to be because God had somehow been displeased. The legislature would then proclaim days of humiliation, mass petitions to God to try and make things right. Evan Morris of Topsfield took a dim view of that practice, saying in 1656, "When some were together keeping a day of humiliation they were howling like wolves and lifting their paws for their children" and "if there had been no members of churches there would have been no need of gallows."

Morris proved fatally prophetic, connecting church members to the gallows like that. He knew all about the Spanish Inquisition, as did everyone. What he didn't know was that the devil would soon bring Essex its own grand infamy, one that also would never be forgotten.

In the Murderers' Playground

The Salem witch hysteria started as a faddish interest in the occult. It quickly grew into the wickedest thing Essex ever knew, resulting in the state-sanctioned execution of nearly two dozen innocents. It was spawned by a cabal of young girls—pretenders—who acted in concert and knew exactly what they were doing. Their heinous, snowballing juggernaut of lies, terror and death was the epitome of evil, and once their maelstrom of malice blew itself out, it was *they* who were shown to be the real witches.

The girls' wickedness didn't stop once the death sentences they inspired were meted out, either. They "followed their victims to the gallows, and jeered, scoffed, insulted them in their dying hours," acting "frivolous, sportive, and gay."[37]

To give the hysteria context, there were only about 15 witchcraft executions *on the entire American continent* in the two hundred years between the first landings of Europeans and 1692, when Essex saw an estimated 140 to 200 accusations in less than a year and the execution of twenty people. There were four more deaths in prison from exposure and disease, and two dogs, considered to be either accomplices or possessed, were also hanged.[38]

Despite post-hysteria statements from some of those directly involved, who plainly admitted wrongdoing, there are some in modern times who have resisted the idea that the whole business stemmed from simple, uncontrolled, wholesale wickedness. One writer, a psychologist, floats the idea of the "exteriorization of the repressed sexual conflicts of women,"[39] which at first sounds vaguely impressive but then reminds us that there is such a thing as showboating psychobabble. Several others point to Salem's feuding Proctors and Putnams and speculate that the witchcraft accusations were encouraged by the girls' parents. There *was* political tension in Salem, and parental influence was of course possible, but that possibility just spreads the wickedness further around. Others suggest ergot poisoning, the ingestion of poisonous alkaloids produced by a fungus that infects rye. Rye was grown locally, and such poisoning might explain the girls' convulsions. But a drought at the time would have reduced the likelihood of the fungus blooming, and if blame is to be laid on some bad rye bread, why would only the accusers be affected when entire families ate from the same loaves?

And if convoluted explanations are to be further pursued, what explains the publicly stated regret of Ann Putnam Jr., prime among the accusers, who, eight years later, at the age of twenty, effectively admitted guilt?

"I desire to lie in the dust and to be humbled for it and earnestly beg forgiveness of all those unto whom I have given just cause of sorrow and offense, whose relations were taken away and accused," she said.[40]

Why would one of the witch judges, Samuel Sewall, ask his minister five years later to read out loud, in Boston's Old South Church, his wish to take "the blame and shame of it"?[41]

Why would twelve members of the jury admit they had been unable to withstand the "delusions" presented to them, claiming that afterward they were "much disquieted and distressed in our minds; and do therefore humbly beg forgiveness," avowing they would not "do such things again on such grounds for the whole world"?[42]

And why would the Great and General Court set aside a day of public fasting in atonement for what had been done?

It was wicked, all right, and no one in Salem—which is inundated on Halloween by so many visitors they bring traffic to a standstill—is allowed to forget it, even though the focus now is mainly on all the "fun" aspects of witches and witchcraft, which constitute much of the "Witch City's" commerce today.

SEEDS OF EVIL, FERTILIZER OF IGNORANCE

Interest in books about prophecy and fortune telling ran high in New England in the winter of 1691–92, especially among children and young people. Throughout Essex County, small, informal circles of adolescents—mostly girls—were preoccupied that winter with divination based on occult experiences.[43]

In the household of Reverend Samuel Parris lived Tituba, a West Indian slave with knowledge of voodoo and the black arts, knowledge that dovetailed nicely with that winter's fad. Tituba, in secret, started teaching Elizabeth Parris and her friends what she knew. The girls soon started to act possessed and to show growing—and markedly similar—symptoms: "running around the house on all fours, barking, and falling into screaming and horrifying convulsions."[44] Then they started "getting into holes, and creeping under chairs and stools, and to use sundry odd postures and antic gestures, uttering foolish, ridiculous speeches, which neither they themselves nor any others could make sense of."[45]

The Salem witch hysteria started in the Parris household with girls throwing inexplicable fits. Artist unknown. *Courtesy Danvers Archival Center.*

Such behavior, the likes of which had never before been seen in Essex, baffled doctors. No one could explain it, and the seventeenth-century belief in witches and the devil was as widespread as the sunrise, so into the vacuum of knowledge and explanation rushed the only "logical" conclusion: demonic possession.

The girls, all more or less neighbors, were Ann Putnam Jr., twelve; Elizabeth Parris, nine, daughter of the Reverend Samuel Parris, in whose church the accusations surfaced; Abigail Williams, eleven, a niece of Reverend Parris; Mary Walcott, seventeen; Mercy Lewis, seventeen, a Putnam servant; Elizabeth Hubbard, seventeen; Elizabeth Booth, eighteen; Susannah Sheldon, eighteen; Mary Warren, twenty, a dissatisfied servant of the Proctors (each of whom were hanged); and Sarah Churchill, twenty, a dissatisfied servant of George Jacobs Jr. (also hanged). They all knew full well—as did every child, by mandate of law—what all the capital crimes were, including witchcraft.

The first to be accused was Tituba, who thus became a victim of the monster she had helped create. Then came Sarah Good, a slovenly, pipe-smoking beggar and an easy target. Then it was the unpopular—and, by reputation, unchaste—Sarah Osborne. All three went to the Ipswich prison, commuting to Salem daily for examinations and questioning, riding on horseback behind the constables. The girls were soon on a roll. Murder was their game, and all of Essex was their playground. They were invited to town after town to hunt suspects, literally pointing out over forty in Andover alone. Their targeting was broadened after they were taught, in sermons, that *anyone* could be a witch; that spelled the end of former Salem minister George Burroughs, a diminutive man deemed suspicious by his prodigious physical strength. He was brought back from Wells, at the eastward, for his trial and hanging.

Witches' physical examinations were held before a fascinated public, hidden from view only when modesty demanded it, with men examining men and women examining women (although a male doctor attended inspections of women). No indignity or physical invasion was spared. The

Fits of "afflicted" girls were acted out in private and in public, as depicted here on a meetinghouse floor. Artist unknown. *Courtesy Danvers Archival Center.*

Examination of a Witch by Tompkins Harrison Matteson, 1853. *Courtesy Peabody Essex Museum.*

violation could not have been more complete, with suspects inspected inside and out, including the nethermost region of Bridget Bishop's crotch, where a "witch's teat"—from which evil spirits were said to take sustenance—was allegedly found. Another woman, Susannah Marine, was deemed suspicious when, in the morning, her breasts "appeared to us very full, the nibs fresh and starting, now at this [afternoon] searching all lank and pendant." Three teats were found on George Jacobs Jr., "which according to our best judgments we think is not natural for we ran a pin through two of them and he was not sensible of it; one of them being within his mouth, [another on] the inside of his right shoulder blade and a third upon his right hip."[46]

The teats, of course, were nothing more than naturally occurring growths, but it was deemed unnatural if their piercings were not felt.

WENCHES AND THEIR "JUGGLING TRICKS"

Once things were under way, it would have been easier for the girls to answer yes to leading questions like whether the accused hurt them or brought them the devil's book to sign, rather than confess their lies. Being revealed as liars would have gotten them in serious trouble, possibly executed themselves. They grew adept at acting possessed, but their convulsions must have taken considerable effort given the strong impression they made. They went on and on, swooning, frothing, gasping for breath, trembling and feigning pain, screeching and screaming in both courtroom and church.

"Those wenches," wrote the accused John Alden, brought in from Boston for questioning, "played their juggling tricks, falling down, crying out, and staring in people's faces."[47]

The girls' pretending was done solo and in concert. When the accused Bridget Bishop lifted her eyes, the girls' eyes rolled up in their sockets. When Bridget shook her head, the girls' heads lolled grotesquely from side to side. During the examination of Sarah Buckley, accusers Mary Walcott, Ann Putnam and Susan Sheldon were all miraculously and simultaneously unable to speak. During the examination of Elizabeth Proctor, Abigail Williams and Ann Putnam came up to strike her with closed fists, but when they drew near, their fists opened and their hands touched her only lightly. Then, wrote Reverend Parris, "Abigail cried out that 'her fingers, her fingers, her fingers burned,' and Ann Putnam took on most grievously, of her head, and sunk down."[48]

But the Reverend Samuel Willard *had* seen this sort of thing before, in Groton in 1671. He hadn't been fooled then, and he wasn't fooled in Salem. Willard was one of the few, , if not the only one, who objected to the witch trials from the beginning. He did so at great personal risk and was indeed promptly accused by the girls of afflicting them. But he had seen similarities in sixteen-year-old Elizabeth Knapp.

"Sometimes she would give sudden shrieks and if wee inquired a reason, would always put it off with some excuse, and then burst forth into immoderate and extravagant laughter," Willard wrote. Elizabeth Knapp also had impeached an upstanding neighbor for causing her violent bodily motions. Willard "never forgot those symptoms nor did he forget Knapp's false accusations."[49]

A few of the Salem girls' lies, documented in *The Salem Witchcraft Papers*, included:

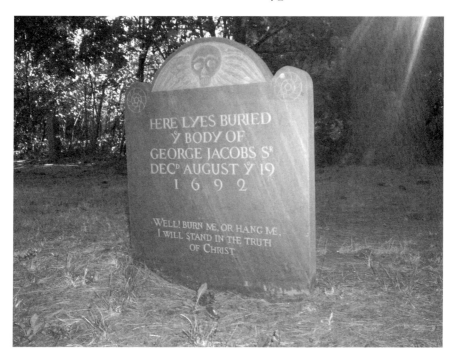

The headstone of George Jacobs Sr., hanged as a witch and buried behind the Rebecca Nurse house in what was Salem and is now Danvers. *Author photo.*

George Burroughs came to her in an apparition one night, claimed Ann Putnam, and "grievously tortured me and urged me to write in his book which I refused." Burroughs also told her his first two wives would soon appear, which they did, saying they wanted vengeance for him murdering them.

Susannah Sheldon said she saw a snake creep over Goody Oliver's shoulder and into her bosom.

Mary Warren, Mary Walcott and Elizabeth Hubbard agreed that if Mary Bradbury looked at them, they would be struck down choking.

Abigail Williams said Sarah Buckley "hath bit me with her scragged teeth a great many times."

Elizabeth Hubbard, adding to the usual allegations of biting, pinching and choking, said Buckley had twisted her neck several times and given her death threats. "I verily believe in my heart that Sarah Buckley is a witch," Elizabeth said.

It would have been natural for the girls to initially enjoy the attention and sympathy, to relish the notoriety and heady excitement and then to succumb absolutely to the seduction of their newfound power. Sending others to their deaths—adults to boot—must have taken on a consuming life of its own. New victims would have been regularly required to keep that kind of excitement alive. Confessions, about fifty, added fuel to the fire. There was great pressure on the accused to confess, pressure from inquisitors, friends and family, because confession was a way out. Not only were all who confessed spared a trial and execution, but they were considered to have taken a step back to godliness. Confessions brought instant relief and the added benefit of "forgiveness" from the girls.

After the hysteria, many confessions were recanted. But Puritans could be as principled—and stubborn—as anyone, and many were loath to admit to something of which they were innocent. And so they were taken away.

BLOOD "OUT OF THEIR NOSES"

In prison, the accused endured "an almost constant stream of visitors, including the curious and the cruel." Jailers tried to force confessions by denying them sleep, forcing them to stand for long periods and using torture. John Proctor was in the Salem jail with his son William and the brothers Richard and Thomas Carrier. Proctor said their jailer tied the young men "neck and heels 'til the blood was ready to come out of their noses."[50] Proctor's son William withstood it; the brothers confessed.

As always in the Puritan era, simply being jailed was torture enough. Ten inmates in Ipswich wrote, after several months, that they were "fettered with

The Witch Jail plaque at 10 Federal Street in Salem. A beam from the jail is in the Peabody Essex Museum two blocks away, viewable by appointment. *Author photo.*

irons this half year and all most destroyed with so long an imprisonment." Whenever possible, witches, considered dangerous inmates indeed, were kept under maximum security in dungeons, "perpetually dark, bitterly cold, and so damp water ran down the walls. They reeked of unwashed human bodies and excrement. They enclosed as much agony as anywhere human beings have lived."[51]

Witches were kept cold, hungry and thirsty, with their limbs weighted and chained to the walls so their specters, or haunts, could less easily escape and wreak havoc. They were treated by wardens and visitors with deliberate cruelty, fair game for sadism since they were already considered enemies of God and mankind.[52]

Most pitiful of all was a prisoner of about five, Dorcas Good, a daughter of Sarah Good, one of the first to be accused. (In prison, Sarah gave birth to another child, who died before her execution, probably from neglect.) As the

The headstone of Rebecca Nurse, hanged as a witch. Her memory is still revered, as the fresh flowers show. *Author photo.*

daughter of a witch, Dorcas Good was a prime suspect. The frightened little girl spent two weeks in the Salem jail, then was taken to Boston, where she was loaded with irons and chained to a wall. As a suspected witch, she would have been treated like the rest—examined, interrogated and made to live with the knowledge she could easily be, and probably *would* be, put to death. She endured it for eight months and was then set free. Her father, William Good, later wrote she "was so hardly used and terrified that she hath ever since been very chargeable, having little or no reason to govern herself."[53]

"Chargeable" means someone had to be paid to care for her. Dorcas, scared out of her wits, didn't care anymore. She had been driven ruinously insane by the wickedness of other girls, some not much older than she.

After all they suffered, death may have been a blessed relief for many. Last farewells to family and friends from the gallows made for powerful and remarkable speeches and sometimes included the condemned's remarkable forgiveness of their accusers. Elderly Mary Esty, the last to die, moved the crowd to tears with a speech that was "as serious, religious, distinct, and affectionate as could well be expressed."[54]

There may have been a point at which it all seemed out of control, and the girls may have become secretly frightened, even crazed, seeing themselves and others slide inexorably into ruin. But whether they wouldn't or couldn't stop feeding the hysteria, they *didn't*, until the governor, seeing his own wife put under suspicion, put an end to it.

WITCHCRAFT ACCUSATIONS AS A CUSTOM

Using the accusation of witchcraft as a weapon in personal, political or business conflicts was nothing new in Essex, and allegations were spun from whole cloth by better storytellers than the girls from Salem.

Peter Pitford of Marblehead said in 1646 that Goodwife James was a witch because he saw her in a boat at sea in the likeness of a cat, and because his garden fruits did not prosper so long as he lived near her.

Bridget Oliver was in court on Christmas Day 1679 for suspicion of witchcraft and, had she not given a bond, would have gone to prison. A man called Wonn, John Ingerson's Negro, said that a month before, when he was in the woods with horses, sledding a load of wood, the horses spooked (presumably near Oliver's house) and ran into a swamp up to their bellies. Witnesses said they never saw the like and thought the horses were bewitched. About a week later, entering his master's barn, Wonn "saw the shape of Goody Oliver upon the beam with an egg in her hand." She then vanished. He ran in fright, told his master and then, afterward, sitting at dinner, saw two black cats. "And we having one black cat of our own and no more I said how come two black cats [are] here, and before my words were well out of my mouth [I] felt three sore grips or pinches on my side that made me cry out, and I had very much pain there and soreness for half an hour," Wonn claimed.

The wildly unpopular John Godfrey (see "Creeps, Meanies and Ne'er-do-wells") was brought to trial when accusations were heaped on him in the mid-1600s by so many Essex residents that their depositions fill a dozen pages in the high court annals. They didn't see him executed, as they fervently wished, but their efforts must have given him pause.

Godfrey was accused of supernaturally damaging people and property and of operating outside the bounds of space and time by being in two places at once. People claimed he caused them to have fits, hear voices, see things and lose the power of speech. Nighttime apparitions attributed to him

The front of the Rebecca Nurse house. *Author photo.*

included a "humble bee," a bear "which ground the teeth and shook the claw," a snake and a cat "thrice as big as an ordinary cat." For a time, if any farm animals fell ill, it was Godfrey's fault.

One couple saw someone they believed to be Godfrey yawn in the Rowley meetinghouse, "and when he did so did see a small teat under his tongue." The same couple said Godfrey was at their house "speaking about the power of witches," saying if witches looked steadfastly upon any creature, it would die, and that if witches were "not kindly entertained the devil will appear."

John Reminton said his horse once began to "start and snort" and the dog with him to "whine and cry." He smelled something sweet and saw a crow flying toward him. The crow had "a very great and quick eye" and a "very great bill." It perched nearby, looking at him, the horse and the dog, and then followed them.

"I began to mistrust and think it was no crow," Reminton said. Then his horse fell, pinning Reminton's leg, and the crow "flew round me several times as if she would light upon me" but didn't. The horse rose, went about four rods and stopped. Reminton was only able to follow on his hands and knees.

"The crow screamed and made a noise like a cat and the hollering of a man." It appeared large, then small and then "flew upon the dog and beat him."

"I was taken very sick and thought I should have died 'til such time the crow left me, and then the dog…rejoyest very much."

When Reminton got home and was resting, Godfrey arrived in a rage, asking how he was. Reminton said, "Pretty well only I was lame with the horse falling on me two days before." To which Godfrey replied, "Every cockating boy must ride, I unhorsed one boy the other day; I will unhorse thee shortly, too."

Susan Roper, fifty-eight, swore that while standing in her doorway in Rowley she saw Godfrey pass by while he was also known to be at Salisbury Court, ten miles distant. Others swore to similar supernatural sightings. John Griffing, twenty-eight, said Godfrey was going toward Newbury at the same time he was also known to be in the Boston prison. Griffing also said that one day he and Godfrey, both heading toward Andover, happened to cross the icebound Merrimack River at the same time, Godfrey on foot and Griffing on horseback. But when Griffing reached Goodman Geag's field, the unmounted Godfrey had arrived *before* him, and Griffing had not seen Godfrey or any of Godfrey's track in the snow en route. Griffin recounted that he had "run my horse all the way to Andover; and the first house I came to at Andover was Goodman Rust's house and when I came in I saw John Godfrey sitting in the corner, and good Rust told me that he had been there so long that a maid…had hung on peas and pork to boil for Godfrey and the peas and pork was ready to boil and the maid was skimming the kettle."

Elizabeth Button said she was home in bed with her daughter by the fire (chimneys often served multiple fireplaces, including those in upstairs bedrooms) when, at about midnight or one o'clock, "there was a great noise…which [I] took to be cattle" but, upon awakening, saw "a shape of a man" sitting in a chair: Godfrey. She would have struck him "but could not put forth my hand." Neither could she "speak nor stir and thus he continued for the space of two hours and I see him three or four times but as soon as I had come to settle myself in the bed he vanished away to my apprehension." Godfrey eventually went "strangely out" because "the door was fast and when I rose in the morning I went to the door and it was fast bolted."

But the campaign to see Godfrey hang was all for naught. As noted before, the high court in Boston found him "suspiciously guilty of witchcraft, but not legally guilty." Once free, he no doubt returned to Essex to continue afflicting the populace with wicked charms, spells and enchantments.

The rear of the Rebecca Nurse house. *Author photo.*

Afterword

Three hundred years after the Puritans, we are now encouraged—and sometimes required—to measure up to new, far higher standards of sensitivity. Yet we still endure atrocities, witch hunts and smothering orthodoxies, it's just that they're all done twenty-first-century style now. Apparently there's no escaping all that, nor the mean, the wicked and the truly disturbed, so we must make the best of a bad situation. But how?

Naturally, when confronted with serious wrongdoing, we steel ourselves, gird our loins and fight back, however futile that might be. But the rest of the time, when the stakes aren't so high, there's an easy defense: view the villains as characters in a black comedy. It's a perspective that can be developed and honed, like any survival skill. Effort is required, and you risk being labeled unserious, but there's always time to fix that. Meanwhile, your complimentary seat at the show comes in wicked handy, whatever the century.

Notes

Introduction

1. *Records of the Court of Assistants, Colony of the Massachusetts Bay, 1630–1692* (Boston: Rockwell & Churchill Press, 1901). Printed under the supervision of John Noble, clerk of the Supreme Judicial Court.
2. Michael Zuckerman, *Peaceable Kingdoms* (New York: Alfred A. Knopf, 1970).

Wicked Deeds and Dire Consequences

3. Thomas M. McDade, *The Annals of Murder, A Bibliography of Books and Pamphlets on American Murders from Colonial Times to 1900* (Norman: University of Oklahoma Press, 1961).
4. Edwin Powers, *Crime and Punishment in Early Massachusetts 1620–1692, A Documentary History* (Boston: Beacon Press, 1966).

Sex: The Good, the Bad and the Loathsome

5. John Winthrop, *Winthrop's Journal, History of New England, 1630–1649*, vols. 1 and 2, edited by James Kendall Hosmer (New York: C. Scribner's Sons, 1908).
6. *Records of the Court of Assistants*.
7. Powers, *Crime and Punishment*.

CREEPS, MEANIES AND NE'ER-DO-WELLS

8. David Brown, *The Case of Giles Corey* (Salem, MA: Essex Institute Historical Collections, 1985).
9. Mary Beth Norton, *In the Devil's Snare: The Salem Witchcraft Crisis of 1692* (New York: Vintage Books, a division of Random House, Inc., 2003).

BRUISERS, BITERS AND BRATS

10. Clifton Johnson, *Old-Time Schools and School-books* (New York: Dover Publications, 1963).
11. Josiah Quincy Jr., *Reports of Cases Argued and Adjudged in the Superior Court of Judicature of the Province of Massachusetts Bay Between 1761 and 1772* (Boston: Little, Brown & Co., 1865).

KILLING, CONFESSION AND THE UNCONSCIONABLE

12. Winthrop, *Winthrop's Journal.*
13. Cotton Mather, *Magnalia, or the Ecclesiastical History of New England* (Hartford, CT: Silus Andrus & Son, 1853).
14. Reverend Joseph Felt, *History of Ipswich, Essex & Hamilton* (Ipswich, MA: The Clamshell Press, 1966).
15. Winthrop, *Winthrop's Journal.*

BRUTAL BUSINESS IN FLESH AND BLOOD

16. Almon Wheeler Lauber, PhD, *Indian Slavery in Colonial Times Within the Present Limits of the United States* (London: Columbia University, 1913).
17. George Wingate Chase, *The History of Haverhill, Massachusetts, 1640 to 1860* (Lowell, MA: published by the author, printed by Stone & Huse, 1861).
18. Lauber, *Indian Slavery.*
19. C.S. Manegold, *Ten Hills Farm, The Forgotten History of Slavery in the North* (Princeton, NJ: Princeton University Press, 2010).
20. Sidney Perley, *The History of Salem Massachusetts* (Salem, MA: Essex Institute, 1924).

21. Manegold, *Ten Hills Farm.*
22. Ibid.
23. Perley, *History of Salem.*
24. Manegold, *Ten Hills Farm.*
25. Claude M. Fuess, ed., *The Story of Essex County* (New York: American Historical Society, 1935).
26. Lauber, *Indian Slavery.*
27. James R. Newhall, *The Essex Memorial for 1836* (Salem, MA: Henry Whipple, 1836).
28. Felt, *History of Ipswich.*
29. Ibid.

The Deadly Wrath of God's Gatekeepers

30. Powers, *Crime and Punishment.*
31. Ibid.
32. Ibid.
33. Ibid.
34. Sidney Perley, *The Essex Antiquarian*, vol. 1 (Salem, MA: Sidney Perley, 1897).
35. Manegold, *Ten Hills Farm.*
36. Richard Gildrie, *The Gallant Life: Theft on the Salem-Marblehead, Massachusetts Waterfront in the 1680s*, vol. 122 (Salem, MA: Essex Institute Historical Collections, October 1986).

In the Murderers' Playground

37. Charles W. Upham, *Salem Witchcraft* (Mineola, NY: Dover Publications, Inc., 2000).
38. Paul Boyer and Stephen Nissenbaum, eds., *The Salem Witchcraft Papers* (Cambridge, MA: Da Capo Press, 1977).
39. Ernest Jones, MD, *On the Nightmare* (London: Hogarth Press, 1931).
40. Frances Hill, *The Salem Witch Trials Reader* (Cambridge, MA: Da Capo Press, 2000).
41. Eve LaPlante, *Salem Witch Judge, The Life and Repentance of Samuel Sewall* (New York: HarperCollins, 2007).

42. Robert Calef, "Witchcraft Confessions," www.piney.com.

43. Boyer and Nissenbaum, *Witchcraft Papers*.

44. Powers, *Crime and Punishment*.

45. Boyer and Nissenbaum, *Witchcraft Papers*.

46. Ibid.

47. Upham, *Salem Witchcraft*.

48. Boyer and Nissenbaum, *Witchcraft Papers*.

49. David Brown, *The Salem Witchcraft Trials: Samuel Willard's Some Miscellany Observations*, vol. 122 (Salem, MA: Essex Institute Historical Collections, July 1986).

50. Hill, *Witch Trials Reader*.

51. Ibid.

52. Ibid.

53. Ibid.

54. Robert Calef, *More Wonders of the Invisible World* (London, 1700).

About the Author

Tom Juergens became an ink-stained wretch in his formative years, taking a quick stab at creating a neighborhood newspaper. He started writing for real newspapers as a Boston University journalism intern, then spent several years as a staff reporter at various New England daily and weekly newspapers, including the now defunct *Beverly Times* and *The Register* on Cape Cod. He has also been published in the *Boston Sunday Globe* and *Offshore*. Other jobs he's held include lineman, carpenter, cabinetmaker, real estate agent, real estate appraiser and paralegal. In between those noneditorial jobs, he has always returned to wordsmithing in one form or another, freelancing as a journalist, corporate writer, technical writer and technical book editor.

After high school he spent nearly a year in Africa, where for a couple of months he drove a forklift, loading and unloading ship cargos. In other travels, he has hitchhiked back and forth across the United States twice and visited both Canada and Europe twice. He also has sailed to the Caribbean twice, once as far as Venezuela, and has served in the United States Coast Guard Auxiliary. Some of his activities and interests include, in no particular order, archery, boating and fishing, gardening, zip-lining, painting and, whenever possible, a bit of adventure. He is grateful to be blessed with what every writer dreams of: the freedom to work on projects of his own choosing. Comments about this book are welcome on its Facebook page, Wicked Puritans, and at wickedpuritans@gmail.com.